D1282638

SEEING
THE
INVISIBLE

*The Art
of
Spiritual
Perception*

A.B. SIMPSON

CHRISTIAN PUBLICATIONS
CAMP HILL, PENNSYLVANIA

Christian Publications, Inc.
3825 Hartzdale Drive, Camp Hill, PA 17011
www.cpi-horizon.com
www.christianpublications.com

Faithful, biblical publishing since 1883

Seeing the Invisible
ISBN: 0-87509-565-8
LOC Catalog Control Number: 94-72622
© 1994 by Christian Publications
All rights reserved
Printed in the United States of America

00 01 02 03 04   6 5 4 3 2

Seeing the Invisible
is an edited version of the Simpson classic
which was formerly published under the title
In the School of Faith.

CONTENTS

INTRODUCTION

The 11th chapter of the epistle to the Hebrews contains the most complete treatise on faith to be found in the Scriptures. It is truly wonderful and grows more clear and comprehensive with each examination. The chapter is introduced by a definition of faith as "The substance of things hoped for, the evidence of things not seen" (11:1, KJV).

This admirable definition teaches us, first, that faith is not hope, not a mere expectation of future things, but a present receiving of that which is promised in a real and substantial way. It is accepting, not expecting.

Second, it teaches us that it is not sight, for it deals with things not seen. The region of the visible is not the land of faith. When a thing is proved by demonstration it is not a matter of faith, but of evidence. Faith asks no other evidences than God's Word and its own assurance. It is the evidence. There is no greater lie than *seeing is believing*. If God has spoken, faith believes where it cannot see, believes what sight and evidence even seem to contradict.

When God said to Abraham, "for I have made you a father of many nations" (Genesis 17:5),

1

there was no sign of it; indeed, the evidence of sight plainly contradicted it. But God said it, and Abraham believed, for faith "calls things that are not as though they were" (Romans 4:17). And so Abraham "considered not his own body now dead" (4:19, KJV) but was strong in faith, giving glory to God, and was fully persuaded that what God had promised, He was able also to perform.

Third, faith recognizes in every case an act of creation. It does not require any material to start with, for it believes in a God who can make all things out of nothing, and therefore it can step out into the seeming void and speak it full of the mighty creations of His power.

In giving the greatest of the promises of the Old Testament, God reveals Himself as the Creator of that which He is promising.

> This is what the LORD says, he who made the earth, the LORD who formed it and established it—the LORD is his name: "Call to me and I will answer you and tell you great and unsearchable things you do not know." (Jeremiah 33:2-3)

There may be no sign of it, no probability of it, no germ of it from which to start, but God is able to make it out of nothing by a word. He needs no foundation work of protoplasm to build His magnificent edifices of worlds. "For he spoke, and it came to be; he commanded, and it stood firm" (Psalm 33:9). Into the soul that has no basis or remnant of goodness but is dead in trespasses and sins, He can speak life and holiness. Into the body, whose constitution is exhausted and its springs of life run out, He can command health and strength. And so faith begins where human hopes and prospects end, and *man's extremity is God's own opportunity.*

Now faith, the apostle declares, is indispensable in order to please God. No wonder; to have anything less is to treat God as if He were unreal and unreliable. That is practical atheism. To trust God less than one of His works is to make His word less sure than a mere material fact of nature and an evidence of the senses.

The reason why God requires our absolute trust is very plain. The ruin of the human race came when the tempter discredited and doubted God's word to our first parents. "Hath God said?" (Genesis 3:1, KJV) was the fountain of all sin. "God hath said" (3:3, KJV) is the foundation, therefore, of our restoration. Only when we thus implicitly believe His word will we love or obey Him. As unbelief stands in front in the first picture of our fallen race, so it leads the procession of the lost in the closing scene in the tragedy of mankind. "The cowardly, the unbelieving . . . their place will be in the fiery lake of burning sulfur. This is the second death" (Revelation 21:8).

"See to it, brothers, that none of you has a sinful, unbelieving heart that turns away from the living God" (Hebrews 3:12).

After having given these general principles

respecting faith, the apostle next proceeds to illustrate them by a series of examples from the Scriptures.

The first seven are taken from the book of Genesis and represent distinct aspects of faith in human life: Abel represents justifying faith; Enoch, sanctifying faith; Noah, separating faith; Jacob, the discipline of faith at length purifying a naturally mean and earthbound soul; and Joseph, the victory of faith, triumphing over injury and innocent suffering.

CHAPTER 1

Abel

Justifying Faith

By faith Abel offered God a better sacrifice than Cain did. By faith he was commended as a righteous man, when God spoke well of his offerings. And by faith he still speaks, even though he is dead. (Hebrews 11:4)

This is the true place for faith to begin. The two men who stand worshiping at the gate of Eden represent the two divisions of mankind—believers and unbelievers.

The earthly man has far more beauty, culture and real effort in his religion. He brings the fruit of his hard toil—the first and best of it. He brings the pure, sweet blossoms of spring and the rich, ripe fruits of summer. Perhaps his altar is festooned with rare beauty and taste and is in favorable contrast to the rude mound of clay on which Abel offers the ghastly and revolting sacrifice of a bleeding, dying, consuming lamb.

But Cain's whole offering was a direct denial of

all that God had said about the curse upon the ground and all its fruits, of the fact of sin and the need of an atoning Savior.

Abel's sacrifice was a simple and humble acknowledgment of all this, and a frank acceptance of God's way of pardon and acceptance.

Believe What God Says about Sin

We see Abel's faith in the acknowledgment of sin manifested in his sacrifice. The first act of faith is to believe what God says about sin. We do not need to try to work up a certain feeling about our sins. It is enough to believe that we are sinners because God says it. Abel did. He took the sinner's place, and instantly he found the sinner's Savior. The publican did, and he "went home justified before God" (Luke 18:14). Cain would not see his sin, and the result was that he fell into deeper sin. He came at last to the other extreme where he had to cry. "My punishment is more than I can bear" (Genesis 4:13).

The devil's first trick is to get us to say, "I have not sinned." Then his last blow is to make us think, "My sin is too great to be forgiven." But humble faith accepts God's judgment upon itself and escapes judgment.

The emperor of France was once leading a foreign king through the prisons of Toulon. As a special act of courtesy, he said, "You can set free any prisoner you please." He spoke to several, but found no one that seemed to deserve it. All were innocent, much abused men. At last he found a sinner, a poor fellow who could only say, "Oh, sire, I am an unworthy man, and am only thankful my punishment is not much worse." At once he set him free, saying, "You are the only man I can find that has anything to be forgiven. You are pardoned by the emperor's command." So the self-righteous miss the great salvation, and the lost are the saved. Thus let us take the place of guilt, and of pardon, through faith in His Word and His blood. He condemns to save. "God has bound all men over to disobedience so that he may have mercy on them all" (Romans 11:32).

Recognize the Divine Provision for Sin

Abel's faith not only recognized the sin, but also the divine provision for it by sacrifice. He did not look at his own character or his own works. It was his gifts that God testified to.

Two men go up to a bank cashier, each holding in his hand a piece of paper. The one is dressed in expensive style, and presents a gloved and jeweled hand. The other is a rough, unwashed workman. But the first is rejected with a polite sentence, and the second receives a thousand dollars over the counter. What is the difference? The one presented a worthless name; the other handed in a note endorsed by the president of the bank. Even so the most virtuous moralist will be turned away from the gates of mercy, and the vilest sinner welcomed in if he presents the name of Jesus.

What can we give to infinite purity and righteousness? We have no gift worthy for God to receive. He has given His Son to us for this very end—that we may give Him as our substitute and satisfaction. He has testified of this gift that in Him He is well pleased, and all who receive Him are "accepted in the beloved" (Ephesians 1:6, KJV). Will we accept the testimony that God is satisfied with Him?

An old Scottish streetcar conductor told me once how he was converted. Riding along in his cart, he was crushed by the load of his sins. The thought kept coming to him, "What shall I give to God to satisfy His claims?" He thought of his reformation, his promises, his services, his tears and everything he could, but all seemed to fail. At last something said, "Offer Jesus." He did, and instantly his soul was filled with the sweet sense of acceptance and blessing.

A Scottish evangelist told me this story. When he was a lad, his father was a shepherd. One morning a lamb was dead. Another lamb was also motherless. He asked his father to give the little orphan to the mother who had just lost her lamb. His father told him she would not have it. He tried again and again, but she would only run from it. At last the father took the dead lamb, and removing its skin, placed it on the living one. Instantly the mother ran to it and began to caress it, and received it as her own. So God covers us with the righteousness of Jesus and loves us with the same love He bears to Him, seeing us only as in Him and accepting us as His very sons and daughters for Jesus' sake.

Abel's faith "commended [him] as a righteous man" (Hebrews 11:4). So we must also believe that we are accepted and justified. Now, this does not merely mean that we are pardoned and exempted from judgment. It means that we are declared and counted righteous utterly and forever justified and placed in the same position as if we had never sinned and had kept all the commandments of God, just as Christ has done.

We get this assurance only by faith. We simply believe the record that God has given us His Son. We may weep and pray, but nothing will bring rest until we simply believe that God has accepted us, justified us and forever loves us in Jesus, and as George Mueller put it, counts each of us "His darling child."

Those who believe this way have peace with God and know that they have eternal life.

The moment the soul accepts its justification and stands clear of the awful shadow of the curse, it springs at once into freedom, love and power. The secret of weak love and strength is feeling faith. A doubt about our perfect acceptance will paralyze all our spiritual power. An Eastern artisan in the employ of a great prince suddenly became an unsteady workman. His exquisite jewelry was marred, and his hand refused to work with its old cunning. His king sent for him and asked the reason. He found that the man was hopelessly in debt and was expecting every day to lose his wife and children as slaves for his indebtedness. The kind prince paid his debt, and in a moment all was right. His hand recovered its spring and his work its beauty. His burden was gone, and he was free. So God sets us free to serve Him, and a full assurance of complete justification is necessary to entire sanctification.

Dr. James, the author of the remarkable volume *Grace for Grace*, and one who was much used of God in personal dealings with burdened souls in all parts of the land, stated as his experience that the greatest hindrance he found to the full acceptance of Christ as an indwelling and sanctifying presence was the prevalence of vague ideas and imperfect assurance respecting absolute and eternal acceptance in Christ.

Do we dare believe that we are absolutely, utterly, eternally accepted in Jesus Christ, in the same sense as He is accepted, and righteous even as He is righteous? Can we believe that our very name before God is: "The LORD Our Righteousness" (Jeremiah 23:6, 33:16)—His own name of ineffable holiness, given to us even as the bride bears the husband's name?

This all comes by a simple act of believing God's testimony. God declares it of us simply because we have accepted Christ's atonement, have believed the declaration and have taken the new place assigned us. The bride stands at the altar and believes the word spoken by the minister, and she fearlessly takes the place of a wife. The sinner believes God's declaration and goes home to his house justified. "Anyone who does not believe God has made him out to be a liar"

(1 John 5:10b). There is one spot on earth covered evermore by the great sentence, "No condemnation." That spot is under the cross of Jesus. The moment we step there and claim the sentence, it is ours, and God cannot break His eternal Word.

A poor criminal stood before an eastern king trembling for his life. In a moment later his head was to be severed from his body. He asked for a drink of water. They brought it, but his hand trembled so that he could not drink. The king cried to him, "Do not be so alarmed; your life is safe until you drink the water." In a moment the glass was smashed on the pavement and the water untasted. Looking boldly up to the king, the criminal claimed his royal word. The king smiled bitterly, but said, "You have fairly won it, and I cannot break my word even to you. Your life is safe."

If the word of a capricious king could shield a wicked man, who will not fly for refuge to the Word of Salvation where every soul may hide? "Whoever believes in him is not condemned" (John 3:18).

CHAPTER 2

Enoch

Sanctifying Faith

> *By faith Enoch was taken from this life, so that he did not experience death; he could not be found, because God had taken him away. For before he was taken, he was commended as one who pleased God. And without faith it is impossible to please God, because anyone who comes to him must believe that he exists and that he rewards those who earnestly seek him. (Hebrews 11:5-6)*

In the patriarch Enoch the human race reached its seventh generation. Seven is the Hebrew number of perfection. The type, in this case of ideal humanity, respects both his character and his destiny. Enoch was the first pattern of holiness since the Fall. And he was the first who rose above the curse of death, giving pledge and promise, in his translation as well as in his teaching, of the glorious immortality that awaits the holy at the second coming of the Lord.

His Character

Enoch's holy life is described by two sentences: "he pleased God" (Hebrews 11:5, KJV) and he "walked with God" (Genesis 5:22, 24).

The divine pleasure or will is ever the standard of holiness. "I always do what pleases him" (John 8:29) was Christ's simple account of His own perfect and blameless character and life. "That you may live a life worthy of the Lord and may please him in every way" (Colossians 1:10) is the apostle's prayer for believers. The very expression is infinitely tender and attractive, showing that God is willing to take real pleasure in our love and obedience, and even delights Himself in the heartfelt sincere attempts of His earthly children to meet His approval. On our part it intimates something more than mere obedience, righteousness and rigid duty. It expresses the spontaneous love that wants to win His smile, not merely escape His judgment. There is a way of regarding and even trying to fulfill the will of God which makes it like a wall of adamant and a bond of iron. But there is a sweeter way which recognizes His will as the tenderest love of a dear Father, a gracious will just adapted to our capabilities and resources, which the sincere and loving heart may be enabled to fulfill so as constantly to please Him.

The little child in learning her ABC's at school may please her teacher as perfectly as the highest graduate in the advanced classes, and yet she cannot even attempt the tasks of the higher class. But she is not expected to; she has only to meet the teacher's will from day to day, and that will is gauged to her progress and ability. So God's will for the humble believer is not a rigid, abstract rule, nor does it demand the same obedience and service as is required of angels and archangels, but it is a tender, gracious plan, adapted to each situation and growth, and unfolding from day to day into all the good pleasure of His goodness.

To please God is the aim of the sanctified man. He does not try to please the world, and perhaps he seems to others a very narrow, disagreeable and one-sided man. He does not live to please himself, and yet no other man has so much real pleasure. Before making a choice or taking a step, he always waits to know God's pleasure, and by keeping his will in the line of God's will, he is not crossed and fretted as others are. His ways are ways of pleasantness and all his paths are peace. He has been sweetly delivered from the spirit of bondage and lives perpetually in the glad sense of God's acceptance and love. To him have come the sweet words: "So now I have sworn not to be angry with you, never to rebuke you again" (Isaiah 54:9b). The smile of God shines evermore upon his path, and he lives in the land of Heph-zibah, the land of which the Lord has said, "[I] will delight in you" (62:4):

Thee to please and Thee to know,
  Constitute my bliss below;

Thee to see and Thee to love,
Constitute my bliss above.

But how can we thus please God? Is it possible
for sinful man ever to please God? Is it not true
that they that are in the flesh cannot please God,
that "The LORD looks down from heaven . . . to
see if there are any who understand, any who seek
God" (Psalm 14:2). But that, "All have turned
aside" (14:3). Is it not true that man's best is as
filthy rags, that the holiest men laid themselves
lowest in the dust and threw themselves wholly
upon the mercy and the grace of God?

Yes, it is all true. And yet it is also true that we
may receive from God that with which we can
please and even wholly satisfy Him, so that we
will stand before Him without fault or blame.
Here is the mystery of godliness of which Jesus is
the wondrous solution.

There is but one Man who ever perfectly pleased
God. It is He of whom the Father said, "This is
my Son, whom I love; with him I am well pleased"
(Matthew 3:17). There is but one way by which we
can perfectly please God, and that is by being so
united to Him, and having Him so indwell us that
He will answer for us in everything, and we can
present Him to God as our perfect offering and
complete life. This secret of justification is that we
accept as a present His blood and righteousness
and are made "accepted in the beloved" (Ephesians
1:6, KJV). The secret of sanctification is that we
receive Him as our inner life and holiness, "who of

God is made unto us . . . sanctification" (1 Corinthians 1:30, KJV). Our holiness is no longer human, but divine, no longer our best attempts, but now His perfect seamless robe. Thus the Father is pleased with us even as He is with Him, and the wondrous prayer is fulfilled, "That the love you have for me may be in them and that I myself may be in them" (John 17:26b).

It is because He is in us now that we are loved with the very same love, for we are now a part of Him.

> So dear, so very dear to God,
>   More dear I could not be,
> The love wherewith He loves His Son,
>   That love He bears to me.

There is no other way of holiness that can ever reach God's high standard or man's low level of perfect helplessness. All else is human; this is divine. It is higher than the best that man can do, yet easier than the least of His own struggles. It is not an attainment, but an obtainment. It is not a task, but a gift. It is "I no longer live, but Christ lives in me" (Galatians 2:20).

Personal Companionship

Now all this is brought out with great beauty in the next expression employed to describe Enoch's holiness. He "walked with God" (Genesis 5:22). His life was a personal companionship with God, not a self-contained and self-sustained righteousness. It was dependent on the divine fellowship and was just as personal as our sweet walk with Jesus now.

For the same Jesus came then at times to the future scene of His toil and suffering and made Himself known. And He was the constant Companion of Enoch's life and walk.

This is the great secret of the Christian life, the mystery hid from ages and generations, but now made manifest unto the saints, "Christ in you, the hope of glory" (Colossians 1:27).

The Christian life is not a wonderful state or a marvelous experience, but a perfect union with Jesus, the living and perfect One.

We do not merely receive grace, but the God of all grace; not merely holiness, but the Holy One; not merely power, but the Mighty One in the midst; not merely wisdom, but the Wonderful Counselor.

The secret of divine holiness is union with Jesus, abiding in Jesus, dependence upon Jesus every moment and for everything. "From the fullness of his grace we have all received one blessing after another" (John 1:16). Our graces are just the transfer of His grace to us. As the transfer picture is laid upon the piece of silk and stamped into its texture with a hot iron, so the Holy Spirit takes the things of Christ and translates them with His burning touch into our lives. We put on His purity. We receive the faith of God. "God has poured out his love into our hearts" (Romans 5:5), and "In this way, love is

made complete among us so that we will have
confidence on the day of judgment, because in
this world we are like him" (1 John 4:17). "My
peace I give you" (John 14:27). "I have told you
this so that my joy may be in you and that your
joy may be complete" (15:11). "All authority in
heaven and on earth has been given to me. . . .
And surely I am with you always" (Matthew
28:18, 20). It is all Christ's grace, power and personal presence.

He comes not as a wealthy friend, advancing a
large sum to aid us in our business, but as a
partner, offering His counsel and His whole capi-
tal. It is received by faith, as the free gift and
finished work of our complete Savior. In one
single act we renounce ourselves, all our sin and
self-confidence, and take Him and His all-sufficiency for every future need. Henceforth our
life is simply putting on Christ more fully from
day to day and ceasing from self. In that blessed
moment of appropriating faith He gives Himself
to us as our complete life, covering all our future
need, and day by day we just enter into it step by
step.

In Him we are now complete. Our whole character, the perfect pattern of the life, is now in
Him in heaven. But now it must be wrought into
us and transferred to our earthly life. This is the
Holy Spirit's work. He takes the gifts and graces
of Christ and brings them into our lives as we
need and receive them day by day. Thus we
receive of His fullness even grace for grace: His

grace for our grace; His supply for our need; His strength for our strength; His body for our body; His spirit for our spirit. He "has become for us wisdom from God—that is, our righteousness, holiness and redemption" (1 Corinthians 1:30).

Much more than mere abstract help and grace, much more even than the Holy Spirit bringing us strength and peace and purity, is the personal companionship with Jesus Himself. Christ really dwells in the heart and walks with us as

> A living, bright reality,
> More dear, more intimately nigh,
> Than even the closest earthly tie.

An American gentleman once visited the saintly Albert Bengel. He was very desirous to hear him pray. So one night he lingered at his door, hoping to overhear his closing devotions. The rooms were adjoining and the doors ajar. The good man finished his studies, closed his books, knelt down for a moment and simply said: "Dear Lord Jesus, things are still the same between us," and then sweetly fell asleep. So close was his communion with his Lord that labor did not interrupt it, and prayer was not necessary to renew it. It was a ceaseless, almost unconscious presence, like the fragrance of the summer garden or the presence of some dear one by our side whose presence we somehow feel, even though the busy hours pass by and not a word is exchanged.

O blessed fellowship divine,
O joy supremely sweet,
Companionship with Jesus Christ,
Makes life with joy replete;
O wondrous grace, O joy sublime,
I've Jesus with me all the time.

His Destiny

For such glorious living there is a worthy consummation.

"Enoch walked with God; then he was no
more, because God took him away" (Genesis
5:24). He became the glorious pattern, not only
of man's perfect spiritual life, but man's physical
immortality and resurrection glory.

And it is indeed doubtful that if those who fail
to enter into the fullness of Christ's grace here
will know the completeness of His glory at His
second coming. The summons to holiness is very
closely linked with the warnings of the advent
and the promise of the marriage feast.

"And with him will be his called, chosen and
faithful followers" (Revelation 17:14). "To him
who overcomes, I will give the right to sit with
me on my throne" (3:21). "Behold, I come like a
thief! Blessed is he who stays awake and keeps his
clothes with him, so that he may not go naked
and be shamefully exposed" (16:15). " 'The wed-
ding of the Lamb has come, and his bride has
made herself ready. Fine linen, bright and clean,
was given her to wear.' (Fine linen stands for the
righteous acts of the saints.)" (19:7-8).

Let us take and let us keep these garments, which are granted to all who will receive and wear them, and let us know the blessedness of these two walks.

"He walked with God" (Genesis 5:22). "They will walk with me, dressed in white, for they are worthy" (Revelation 3:4).

CHAPTER 3

Noah

Separating Faith

By faith Noah, when warned about things not yet seen, in holy fear built an ark to save his family. By his faith he condemned the world and became heir of the righteousness that comes by faith. (Hebrews 11:7)

The great lesson of Noah's life is the necessity of separation from the world. He did not save it, although he tried to for 120 years, but he at least bore witness against it and left it without excuse.

When George Whitefield was asked by his roommate, in a country inn, what he had gained by leaving his bed and going down into the barroom to warn the patrons there, to be met only by their mockery and scorn, he answered: "I have gained a good conscience and left them without excuse." Our business is not always to save, but simply to be faithful witnesses.

The cause of the deluge was that very thing

which is bringing about the last apostasy, that is, the mingling of the Church and the world. God told His children at the beginning that there must be enmity between the two seeds, the woman's and the serpent's. He soon made the truth terribly plain in the deadly hate of Cain and the murder of Abel. In Seth's day the races were kept separate, for we read of his family: "Then began men to call themselves by the name of Jehovah" (Genesis 4:26, margin). But in the days of Noah the fatal compromise had fully begun. The sons of God, or the godly race, saw the daughters of men—that is, no doubt, the seed of Cain—that they were fair, and, thinking only of their own earthly desire and not of God's will, "they married any of them they chose" (6:2). The offspring of these unions was a race marked by splendid physical culture, but equally charac- terized by depravity and moral degradation. These giants in stature were monsters of wicked- ness, and their violence filled the earth with blood. One of the earliest discoveries of geologi- cal specimens of the human race shows a man of gigantic stature, but by his side lies a woman with her skull crushed in by a murderous blow which corresponds exactly with God's picture of primi- tive man.

This is the result of the devil's unholy alliance between the Church and the world. It is filling the Church once more, and it will bring another flood—*a flood of fire*. Its forms are *innumerable*. The world invades the home, the sanctuary, the

pulpit, the seminary, the whole fiber and structure of modern religion. It is the devil's snare,
and its evil touch is forbidden by God in the
Bible's most urgent and reiterated warnings.
When Balaam could not destroy Israel by his
curse, he ensnared them by the world's fascinations:

> Do not love the world or anything in the
> world. (1 John 2:15)

> Therefore come out from them
>   and be separate, . . .
> Touch no unclean thing,
>   and I will receive you.
>   (2 Corinthians 6:17)

> What fellowship can light have with dark-
> ness? What harmony is there between
> Christ and Belial? What does a believer
> have in common with an unbeliever? (6:14-
> 15)

These are some of God's signals over the inviting
archways of the forbidden land. And yet Christians walk coolly past them, only to awaken to
their danger when it is too late to return. They
are like the eagle that sat down on the frozen
ground to feed upon its prey, and when it would
have risen, found its great wings so frozen to the
ice that it could never rise again, but perished beside its costly pleasure. Like the ship that sailed

so close to the current that it was impossible to stem the awful tide that drove it over the abyss, so Christian men and women are trifling with forbidden things until they have neither heart nor strength to rise to their heavenly calling.

A Christian has no more business in the theater than Jesus has. A Christian father has no more right to give his child's hand to an unbeliever, or a Christian minister to unite them in marriage, than to sell her into a Hindu harem. And yet such ideas are considered obsolete and narrow; and not only does the membership of the church patronize the broadest and most popular theaters, but the Sunday school picnic and the religious entertainment are vying with the drama for popular attraction. All this is bringing in the latter days. The end is judgment. The only remedies are the faith and faithfulness of Noah. Never will the world be saved by our compromise with it, but only by our standing on God's level and lifting men up to our side.

We Need Noah's Faith

We can only take this place of separation when we have Noah's faith. It was because Noah had found a better world that he let the old world go. The raven will settle down upon the carrion feast of the flood, but the dove will take the olive leaf as her pledge of a future world of peace and blessedness, and wait in the ark until the evil days are past for freedom and inheritance.

A gardener had a willow tree which he tried in

vain to make grow in symmetry. It would send out all its branches only on one side, and in spite of all his twisting and pruning it grew all crooked and lopsided. At last he found the reason. There was a little subterranean stream running on that side of the tree, from which it drew all its nourishment, and it grew toward the source of its life. He immediately changed his tactics. He stopped pruning and tying, and just took his spade and dug another channel on the other side of the tree, directing the water from its old course and supplying it on the neglected side. And before another year had passed, the tree had wholly changed its form. It had sent out its roots below and its branches above toward the welcome waters, and had grown straight and beautiful without an effort. This is the secret of the great Husbandman, too.

> Since, then, you have been raised with Christ, set your hearts on things above, . . . Set your minds on things above, not on earthly things. For you died, and your life is now hidden with Christ in God. When Christ, who is your life, appears, then you also will appear with him in glory. (Colossians 3:1-4)

The Apostle Peter, in speaking of Noah, says a most singular thing about him. He says his household was "saved through [by, KJV] water" (1 Peter 3:20). Most persons would think they were saved *from* water. But it was not so. "And this water symbolizes baptism that now saves you also . . . by the resurrection of Jesus Christ" (3:21). The water of the deluge, like baptism—which is a similar figure—was significant of our death and resurrection with Christ. Noah was saved from the flood of the world which had almost engulfed his family, by that other flood of water. And so we are saved from the world by the cross of Jesus Christ by which the world is crucified unto us and we unto the world. It is only as we really know in our spirit the meaning of that death (and let our spirit die with Him to all the old natural life of the flesh and rise with a new nature, even His own, to a new inheritance, even His kingdom and His throne) that we can rise above it. It can attack us no more. We are not of the world, even as He is not of the world. Just as a magnet, drawn through a box of earth mingled with iron fillings, leaves the earth and draws to it every particle of iron without an effort, so the heavenborn spirit springs to Christ, and the earthly neither know nor care for His call.

> Rise my soul and stretch thy wings,
>   Thy better portion trace;
> Rise from transitory things
>   Toward heaven, thy native place.
>
> Rivers to the ocean run,
>   Nor stay in all their course;

Fire, ascending seeks the sun—
  Both speed them to their source.

So a soul that's born of God
  Pants to see His glorious face,
Upward tends to His abode,
  To rest in His embrace.

We need not go out of the world to be
separated from it. The water spider makes its
home beneath the surface of that pool, but no
drop of water ever touches its soft and downy
coat. From the upper world it takes down a
globule of air and anchors it underwater—a white
bubble of buoyant air which displaces the water—
and in the center the spider makes its nest, living
beneath the waves but breathing in the air of the
upper world. So can we be shut in by God's Holy
Spirit like an encompassing world of light and
life, beneath the dark waves of the world and sin,
but separated even from its touch in the secret of
His presence.

CHAPTER 4

Abraham

Obedience of Faith

By faith Abraham, when called to go to a place he would later receive as his inheritance, obeyed and went, even though he did not know where he was going. By faith he made his home in the promised land like a stranger in a foreign country; he lived in tents, as did Isaac and Jacob, who were heirs with him of the same promise. For he was looking forward to the city with foundations, whose architect and builder is God.

By faith Abraham, even though he was past age—and Sarah herself was barren—was enabled to become a father because he considered him faithful who had made the promise. And so from this one man, and he as good as dead, came descendants as numerous as the stars in the sky and as countless as the sand on the seashore. . . .

By faith Abraham, when God tested him, offered Isaac as a sacrifice. He who had

received the promises was about to sacrifice his
one and only son, even though God had said to
him, "It is through Isaac that your offspring
will be reckoned." Abraham reasoned that God
could raise the dead, and figuratively speak-
ing, he did receive Isaac back from death.
(Hebrews 11:8-12, 17-19)

A braham has been called the Columbus of
Faith—not because he was the only one
who ever traversed these great and trackless was-
tes, but because he was the first. So wide and
comprehensive was the range of his faith and its
trials and triumphs that God Himself called him
"the father of all who believe" (Romans 4:11).

His faith shines out in seven rainbow-like hues
of distinct and glorious luster.

Faith Obeying God's Commands

"By faith Abraham, when called . . . obeyed"
(Hebrews 11:8). Faith meets us in the very beginning as an act of obedience, and thus God ever
regards it and enjoins it. It is not an option with
us whether or not we will believe God's Word,
but "this is his command: to believe in the name
of his Son, Jesus Christ" (1 John 3:23). This
makes the act of faith at once imperative and yet
simple and easy. It is imperative because, if He
has commanded, we have no choice but to obey;
easy, because if He has commanded, He is
responsible to carry us through and fulfill His
promise to us. God is as much bound by His

Word as we are. Therefore, whenever faith can clearly know that He has spoken, all it has to do is to lay the whole responsibility on Him and go forward. "God is not a man, that he should lie, nor a son of man, that he should change his mind. Does he speak and then not act? Does he promise and not fulfill?" (Numbers 23:19).

Faith Trusting God in the Dark

"Abraham . . . went, even though he did not know where he was going" (Hebrews 11:8). The next stage is faith without sight. When we can see, it is not faith, but reason. In crossing the Atlantic, I was struck with the illustration of this very principle of faith. We saw no path upon the sea or sign of the shore. And yet day by day, we were making our path upon the chart as exactly as if there were a great chalk line upon the sea. When we came within 20 miles of land we knew where we were as exactly as if we had seen it all 3,000 miles ahead. How had we measured and marked our course? Day by day our captain had taken his instruments, and looking up to the sky had fixed his course by the sun. He was sailing by the heavenly, not the earthly, lights. So faith looks up and sails on, by God's great Sun, not seeing one shoreline or earthly lighthouse or path upon the way. Often its step seems to lead into utter uncertainty, even darkness and disaster. But He opens the way, and often makes such midnight hours the very gates of day.

Once in going down an Alpine path, the

travelers found their way completely closed. The little path down the mountain torrent suddenly ended in a vast ice cliff, under which the torrent plunged and disappeared in darkness. What were they to do? Suddenly the guide leaped into the stream and bade his companions follow. For a moment there was terrible darkness and fear. Then they were carried by the stream under the ice mountain, and a moment later, gently flung on the banks of green in the valley of Chamonix. So often faith has to go right into the darkness and find God and glorious deliverance in what seems the very death plunge. In many a step of faith the way seems to close completely, and just when all seems threatened with disaster, God delivers. The more fully God purposes to teach us faith, the more will He shut us up to Himself alone and shut out of our view the human sources of help which He holds at His command until we have learned to trust Him fully without either sight or sign of help.

Faith Believing God's Definite Promise

For a while Abraham had only God's general promise of guidance as he went on from day to day. But before long the promise grew more specific, and at last it was clear and plain—a star of fixed magnitude upon the sky of his future, the promise of an inheritance and a child. Faith changed from a simple trust in His wisdom and love to a specific expectation. Here he had to stand, and believe, and wait for God to fulfill.

Here we, too, must follow Him. Our day, at first unmarked, save by His presence as He goes before, will become more clear and definite; prayers and promises will populate it with real forms, and, having claimed, we must learn to count them real, and call those "things that are not as though they were" (Romans 4:17). This is the faith which justifies us. It believes that God does forgive and save and will help. This is the faith that claims and receives real answers to prayer. This is the faith that claims divine healing. It is not merely a general trust that God will do what is best, but a specific confidence that He will do the thing we ask Him, if that thing is one that He has promised in His Word.

Faith Confessing Its Confidence

Abraham no sooner believed the promise of his seed than he had to change his name. God commanded him at once to take, in the sight of all men, a name that literally signified his great and stupendous claim. This must have been very hard, for it involved, no doubt, an explanation to the people who knew him of the meaning of the change, and a humble confession of what to many must have seemed the most ridiculous fanaticism. But Christ ever asks us, "Who do you say I am?" (Matthew 16:15). Faith must always set its seal to it that God is true, and say "the Lord is my helper" (Hebrews 13:6).

Faith will die without confession; but a true and humble acknowledgment commits and confirms it. If the healed demoniac had not gone home to his friends and put himself on record for Christ he probably would have fallen; and if Simon Peter had fearlessly followed with Christ's little band he would not have denied Him. We must not merely believe, but we must even call the "things that are not as though they were" (Romans 4:17), and take the witness stand for God in all that He has called us to.

Faith Yielding up the World for a Better Inheritance

It was not long before Lot, with his earthly spirit, began to contend for the best of the land. Abraham let him have it, and that same night God appeared to Abraham and told him it was all his own, Lot's portion as well as the rest. Not long after, even Lot had to look to Abraham to defend the portion that he chose. The man of faith can let the present world go because he knows he has a better; but even as he lets it go God tells him that all things are his because he is Christ's.

Faith Contending against the Devil for Its Full Inheritance

Abraham would not contend with Lot for the best pastures, but when the kings of the east invaded Canaan and set their foot on his inheritance, he rose up in the might of divine faith, and in the most chivalrous exploit of ancient times, defeated and drove them from the land and rescued Lot and his family. Faith can fight as well as yield, but it always fights against the enemies of God, never against its brethren. God wants us to know and use the aggressive and authoritative act of faith which claims, commands and overcomes, and says to this mountain: " 'Go, throw yourself into the sea,' . . . it will be done" (Matthew 21:21).

Faith Bearing the Test and Entering into Rest and Resurrection Life

At length the very promise he had received, claimed and confessed, seemed challenged. Isaac, the link of all the promise, had to be given up. Was it then a mistake that in Isaac all the seed was to come? No; not for a second did he question. Isaac might even die, but God could not break His word. It would all come, even if Isaac was raised from the dead. This was really what Abraham looked for. It was his faith, therefore, not only his obedience and love that was tested. And it was because he believed that God would give him faith that Abraham was able to give Isaac up. So God would have us stand in the most trying hours, knowing that He cannot lie, and so fully trusting Him that we give up our very blessings to His hand and our very promises to His keeping, knowing that "he who promised is faithful" (Hebrews 10:23).

Such trials only bring out the richer preciousness and overcoming power of faith. In the desert there is a flower which blooms only when the winds blow. Then amid fierce blast and heat, a little star-like flower comes out on every stem. So faith blossoms when the winds of trial blow the fiercest. Faith finds its very soil and nurture in the difficulties and testings of life. May the Lord so fill us with the faith of Abraham that God cannot only give, but give back, the Isaacs of His love, and lead us into the rest of his closing days, as he waited for the fullness and fruitage of a life of faith which made him worthy to be called the friend of God.

CHAPTER 5

Isaac

The Patience of Faith

By faith Isaac blessed Jacob and Esau in regard to their future. (Hebrews 11:20)

The life and character of Isaac is one of the quiet pictures of the Old Testament. He is an actor in no great or exciting events, but moves in a placid, passive sphere, acted upon rather than acting, and submissive and suffering rather than aggressive and strong.

And yet this gentle, shrinking man was, more than any of the patriarchs, the chosen type of Jesus Christ and the example for us of the very hardest and highest thing in our Christ life—the death of self and the love that suffers long and endures all things.

God has appointed our path to life through the gates of death. The Great Master and Martyr said of Himself and us, "unless a kernel of wheat falls to the ground and dies, it remains only a single seed. But if it dies, it produces many seeds" (John

12:24). Our Christian life is not the cultivating but the cutting down of the old plant, and the engrafting of a new nature born from above and rooted in Christ. Anything less than this must end in failure and a far worse death. Of the old natural and Adamic life it can be said uncompromisingly, as the old general said of the opposing army: "Soldiers, there is the enemy; if you don't kill them, they'll kill you." There can be no compromise. The old man must die in us, or we will die with him forever.

Four Symbolic Deaths

When God led His people out of Egypt He caused them to pass through four deaths in symbol: 1. the Red Sea, the type of death to the world; 2. the Jordan, the type of death to the old religious life; 3. circumstances, the type of death to the flesh in its vital and self-propagating principle; and 4. Joshua's vision of the Captain of the Lord's Host and his absolute prostration at His feet, a type of death of our confidence and strength for the work of God.

There is no finer example in the Bible of the necessity of a complete self-crucifixion than Jonah. In the first instance his intense self-will completely unfitted him for service and led him on to daring and open disobedience. God, almost literally, had to kill him and bury him before He could use him at all. Certainly his terrible funeral was intended as a picture of our death to self. Even after he arose it was but too evident that the old man was not yet dead. He did not now disobey, but he left enough of his own wretched shadow across his work, and left his miserable, morbid and murmuring figure under the Assyrian sun as a memorial of one whom God might have made the most illustrious prophet of the ages if only he could have been rid of self.

The Lesson of Isaac's Life

Now, this is the lesson of Isaac's life, the death of self and the life of meekness, patience and lowliness.

His first experience as a child was one of painful trial. He was the younger brother and rival of Ishmael, and was persecuted and scorned by him for his faith. At length Ishmael was cast out and Isaac was delivered from that which was a type of the earthly and fleshly man.

But soon he had to die in a much more radical way. We hear much of the obedient faith of Abraham, but we do not think enough of the act of Isaac in yielding up himself. That was a real death on Mount Moriah, the death of his will forever. This is ever the real self which has to be slain. That scene was not only the foreshadowing of Christ's death, but also of yours and mine. Have you then died? Will you? It is not your vices, your tempers, your sins, but yourself. Will you die?

We next see him in the same beautiful aspect in the yet deeper life of his heart and affections, in connection with his marriage.

There is no part of our life which so influences our character and destiny and so tests our real consecration as the termination of our affections. Therefore, God has from the beginning made the most stringent provisions for the regulation and government of marriage. Knowing so well that the entangling of our hearts with unholy alliances will draw them away from Him, our tenderest earthly ties must be linked with His love and blessing. He has strictly forbidden the intermarriage of His people with the wicked or worldly, and requires that their choice should be made in and for Him, and never with the daughters of men that brought about the corruption that preceded the deluge. It was the intermarriage of the Israelites with the Canaanites that led them back to bondage in the days of the Judges. It was Solomon's marriages with heathen wives that corrupted his heart and destroyed his kingdom. Many a life has been blighted and separated from God by a selfish and worldly friendship, and many a consecration sealed and consummated in the sacrifice of an affection that could not be held in harmony with the will of God. Many a sacrifice might have been saved by waiting to know God's will before making a choice. This was just what Isaac did. He suspended his will to the will of God and allowed God to choose for him the companion of his life and the mother of God's future Israel.

It was a beautiful instance of self-renunciation, and it was honored by God's most signal inter-

position in directing the instrument employed—
the faithful Eleazer. Eleazer stands in this, as his
name signifies, as a type of the Holy Spirit, just as
Abraham does for the Father. It is not meant that
in a matter so delicate and important we are to
submit our hearts and happiness to the decision
of any man or woman, but committing our way
and will to the Father, and holding our hearts
subject to His choice, we are to ask and expect
the Holy Spirit to guide us and form all our attachments, friendships and relationships only on
and for Him. This is true self-renunciation. The
ties thus formed will be intensely more strong,
pure and happy than mere earthly passion can
ever find. The heart conscious of God's eternal
choice and kindly approval can love with a
freedom and intensity which earthly friendship
cannot know. The affections kindled by the Holy
Spirit glow with the calm, deep strength of a
divine love, and the gift dedicated to God will be
made by God a tenfold blessing to the heart that
consecrates it.

But this, let us remember, was the meekness
not of nature but of faith. It was because Isaac
trusted implicitly that he committed his happiness absolutely to God. We cannot commit our
lives to God unless we trust Him to do better for
us than we could for ourselves. So let us trust
Him.

Our times are in Thy hand:
    O God, we trust them there,

Our hearts, our lives, our all we leave
　　Entirely to Thy care.

Our times are in Thy hand,
　　Why should we doubt or fear?
A Father's hand will never cause
　　His child a needless tear.

Faith and Patience in the Trials of Life

We next see Isaac's faith and patience in relation to the trials of life. Famine drove him from his home to take refuge with Abimelech, king of Gerar. Next his wife was threatened with dishonor and in an hour of weakness he repeated the sin of his father Abraham and denied her. God blessed him with great prosperity, but like many other rich men, the Philistines envied him and at last asked him to leave them. Meekly and patiently he went away and left even the wells of water which he had opened in the valley. Again he opened the wells, and again he yielded and moved away. A third time he moved to a new home and dug again the wells, which to a desert dweller are more than food to us; and yet again contention vexed his patient spirit and compelled him to remove once more. The fourth time the wells were unmolested, and patience had its reward. The Philistines were subdued by a man with whom they could not quarrel, and his enemies were killed with the sword of kindness. The Lord made room for him and brought him into a large place, and soon his old enemies came to him requesting his alliance and declaring, "We saw clearly that the LORD was with you; so we said, 'There ought to be a sworn agreement between us' . . . Let us make a treaty with you that you will do us no harm, just as we did not molest you but always treated you well and sent you away in peace. And now you are blessed by the LORD" (Genesis 26:28-29). That was worth a hundred wells.

Yes, consistency and meekness will win the day. "Blessed are the meek, for they will inherit the earth" (Matthew 5:5). This is the fruit of faith. It can trust the Lord to fight its battles and vindicate its innocence, and it can wait its time, through shame and loss and the triumph of wrong and pride. The men and women who fight so hard for themselves have no God to fight their battles or no faith in Him for it. But let us who know His name put our trust in Him. Let us who know His love, faithfulness and power stand still and see the salvation of our God.

> Leave to His love and might
> 　　To choose and to command.
> So shall thy soul with rapture know
> 　　How wise, how strong His hand.

Isaac's last trials were with his children. He himself was to blame for many of them. Had he believed as fully as his wife the divine promises and predictions that preceded their birth, he would have better known the will of God for them, and been saved the vain struggle to carry out his own preconceived ideas. Looking at the natural rather than the spiritual, he set his heart upon the firstborn, the bold, manly, generous Esau. Ah, Isaac, you must die once more to all the pride of earth and all your ideas and preferences must be given up for God's will and word about your children. How many parents have died to the world in themselves but not in their offspring! How many plans and prospects they have that are not of God! How often God has to humiliate and disappoint them in the very objects of their idolatrous love or worldly compromise! So Isaac had to see his plans shattered, hear the bitter cry of his eldest born, and give the covenant blessing to Jacob. But when he saw the divine will he struggled no more; he acquiesced at once, and added his own amen, "and indeed he will be blessed!" (Genesis 27:33).

Isaac had to die more than once, but when he did, he did it gloriously. He plunged right into the will of God and there was no more about it. The trial did not soon end, but the obedience was complete. Esau continued to be a deep trial by his worldly marriages and earthly minded life. Jacob went forth for more than a score of years, to see his face no more until both he and Esau gathered at his dying bed. The shadow of a deadly hate between brothers filled his heart, no doubt, with keenest bitterness, but not once do we see a shadow upon his spirit. Patience had, no doubt, its perfect work. He became in age as well as youth the type of the suffering Savior, the meek and lowly in heart, and the pattern of those graces which God burns into willing and waiting souls by fiery suffering. Not "love does much or says much," but "Love is patient" (1 Corinthians 13:4). Or love "always protects, always trusts, always hopes, always perseveres" (13:7).

"What has all this to do with faith?" you ask. Ah, this is the work of faith. "If [your brother] sins against you seven times in a day, and seven times comes back to you and says, 'I repent,' forgive him" (Luke 17:4). What was the disciples' response to that? "Increase our faith!" (17:5). Why did they not say: "Lord, increase our love"? Because they saw that only stupendous faith could bring such love; only Christ's own love received by faith could thus triumph. And so the apostle wrote to the Colossians: "strengthened with all power according to his glorious might so that you may have"—strength to work?—no! "So that you may have great endurance and patience, and joyfully [give] thanks to the Father" (1:11-12).

That is the patience of faith, and it can only come through His generous power, and the faith that works by love.

So may He baptize us into the spirit of Isaac, the spirit of Christ, the patience of faith.

CHAPTER 6

Jacob

The Discipline of Faith

By faith Jacob, when he was dying, blessed each of Joseph's sons, and worshiped as he leaned on the top of his staff. (Hebrews 11:21)

The most illustrious of all the patriarchs, the one who humanly speaking founded the Hebrew nation and gave his name for all time to Israel, the literal progenitor of the tribes of God's chosen people, was naturally the least noble and attractive of all the patriarchs. In fact, he was the meanest and most selfish of all the characters of this series. Twelve hundred years later the prophet Isaiah speaks of him as the "worm Jacob" (Isaiah 41:14), and the figure well expresses his insinuating and undermining nature. Yet, out of this wretched material God made His own great prince to show to us poor sinners what grace can do with a sinful man if he will but receive its discipline. Let us look at the five chapters of his history.

His Choice

He chose the birthright and the blessing which it involved. He set his heart upon the covenant blessing of his race. As selfish, grasping and intriguing were the means he took to accomplish his purpose, the one thing which eternally distinguishes him from the earth-born and earthly minded Esau is this: he appreciated and claimed, with every fiber of his being, the great, the one all-embracing prize of God's covenant promise, which Esau profanely despised and cheaply bartered away. In spite of all his other defects, the eye of God saw this one thing—the preference, the choice of his will for spiritual and divine things. Thus he represents the first germ of the spiritual nature in any soul, the determination of the will, the direction of the heart, the singleness of the purpose, the value a man places on eternal things.

Esau is superficial, transient, sordid, earthly minded, animal. His highest good is the present gratification; his horizon stretches only to the setting sun. His deepest desire and aspirations are the instincts, passions, wants of his animal or physical nature. He is impulsively generous, frank and affectionate; but it is on animal instinct. He is the fleshly man. " 'Look, I am about to die,' Esau said. 'What good is the birthright to me?' " (Genesis 25:32). That was the very time when faith would have looked out on the eternal profit, or claimed that, with such a promise, he should not die till the birthright covenant was fulfilled.

But Jacob saw "a land that stretches afar" (Isaiah 33:17), and sprang to meet it. He sold all that he had for the pearl of great price, and grasped with both hands the priceless blessing of which his fond mother had often told him, but whose full significance he might only yet dimly comprehend. But this he knew, that it was linked with all the promises of God and all the hopes of his race. God loved him for this choice. It was the mightiest thing in his life.

The mightiest thing in any life is a will that sees the heavenly prize and gets its hand upon it to let go no more, to claim it and hold at any cost the great inheritance. It was this same mighty will which afterward at Peniel held fast to the angel presence and cried: "I will not let you go unless you bless me" (Genesis 32:26). To choose God, His promise, His inheritance, His blessing, and to let heaven and earth pass away before we relinquish the claim is the very essence of faith. It was of this He said to Martha, "Mary has chosen what is better, and it will not be taken away from her" (Luke 10:42). It was of this He said to the Canaanite woman: "Woman, you have great faith! Your request is granted" (Matthew 15:28).

Jacob's faith was not complete. Had it been he would not have begun to work out so cunningly his chosen destiny, but would have trusted God to do what He had promised before his birth. All this he had to slowly and painfully learn. He had to be saved from the scheming, supplanting, restless spirit of Jacob. But he had the germ, a single aim, a fixed will and a perfect heart toward the covenant blessing, and God could well afford to hew and polish and cut away the rest.

As to Esau, there was nothing to prune and purify. The roots of his nature were all in the world. He had not one chord in common with the heart of God. He was, perhaps, handsome, generous and large-hearted, but so is many a dumb creature that knows not God. A noble dog, a generous horse, a fond mother-bird are attractive too, but they are only animated clay, and for man to lift his eyes and heart no higher is to be lost forever. The world is full of Esaus, fine people in their way, but "their destiny is destruction, their God is their stomach . . . Their mind is on earthly things" (Philippians 3:19).

His First Revelation

He had chosen God, through his mother's teachings, no doubt, and through the simple letter of the Word. But he had not yet seen God for himself. The Most High had not yet spoken to his heart. He was a good deal like the soul that has given itself to Christ on simple faith and choice, but has not yet received any deep experiential sense of eternal things. But now the time for this had come. As often happens, it came in the dark and trying hour.

Separated, for the first time, from his home and his mother's tender love through the consequences of her artifice and his own, he laid his head on a stony pillow—which might well represent the feelings of his heart—and went to sleep. In his dreams the Lord met Jacob in His first revelation of covenant grace. A ladder set up on the earth, its top reaching to heaven, was the fitting figure of his own high purpose. He, too, had set his ladder no lower than the skies, and God met him at the top as the God of Abraham and Isaac. God gave him in covenant the promises he had claimed, pledging to him His constant presence until all His promised will would be finished. "I am with you and will watch over you wherever you go, . . . I will not leave you until I have done what I have promised you" (Genesis 28:15). Jacob awoke with a solemn sense of God's immediate presence, and while his words expressed the deepest reverence and the same inflexible purpose, yet there was all the distance and the dread of the yet unsanctified heart. "How dreadful is this place!" (28:17, KJV) is the language of the soul that does not yet know its sonship. But he was a true servant, and knew henceforth that his choice was sealed. The God of Abraham was his Lord. He knew that the covenant blessing had become his own, and that the angels of God's providence henceforth would encompass his path.

For us the vision means more than Jacob saw. That ladder is the revelation of Jesus Christ as the heavenly way, through whom God becomes our covenant Father and all heaven's blessings are made our inheritance. Has our faith claimed the glorious revelation, and have our feet begun to climb the blessed ascent?

Deeper Revelation and Consecration

More than 20 years passed by, and Jacob had grown but little, if any, in his spiritual life. He was just like us all, content in the low plane of spiritual life with which we began. He allowed idolatry to be retained by his wives; he continued to plot and scheme to outwit even the crafty Laban; he accumulated a real fortune in herds and flocks; and perhaps his heart had begun to rest in the prosperity of his outward estate.

But God let new troubles gather around him, and as he returned once more to his old Canaan home, the most terrible peril of his life confronted him. Esau with an armed band was coming to meet him, and all the treasured bitterness of a quarter of a century, no doubt, had been waiting for the opportunity of terrible vengeance. It was the crisis of his life, and all his policy and shrewdness were insufficient to meet it. Still he did all that tact can do. He sent on a costly present to Esau and separated his little band in the safest way he could contrive. Then, with a desolate sense of his utter helplessness, he fell at the feet of God. Again Jacob saw the midnight of life, and again the dawn of a brighter morning. The hour of despair became the hour of self-renunciation and divine victory. Alone with God at Jabbok's ford, he wrestled in all the strength of his despair, and when his strength was gone and he sank under the withering touch of the angel's hand, he found the secret of power and exchanged his strength for God's omnipotence.

It was not that the mighty wrestlings of his prayer were wrong, or are wrong for all—all things are born in the throes of travail—but it was that he should learn that another than he was wrestling too. "A man wrestled with him" (32:24). And when he yielded himself up to that Presence in the submission of perfect trust, then came the fullness of God's working and God's victorious love. Ah! We too must learn that the secret of our deepest desires after God is His own prevenient grace; the spring of our mightiest doing and praying must be His doing and praying in us, so that we will ever say with Paul, "To this end I labor, struggling with all his energy, which so powerfully works in me" (Colossians 1:29). Jacob rose from that hour a new man.

"Your name will no longer be Jacob, but Israel, because you have struggled with God . . . and have overcome" (Genesis 32:28).

Not a word was said about Esau or the trouble that had almost distracted him before. God had not even mentioned it, and Jacob had lost all thought of it in another Presence. When he had God Himself, he had all things. When the soul reaches the heart of things in Him, all its cares and questions flee. It is not even that He speaks of them, but He Himself is the answer to them all. Perhaps the trouble was the occasion that brought us to Him; perhaps we came thinking of little else and with very little thought of Him, but we go away lost in a Presence that bears us and our burden, too. It is well to bring our difficulties, even our very minor ones, to Him; for an aching finger is as good an occasion to know Him as the largest issue of life. But it is the Blesser and not the blessing, it is the Lord and not the deliverance that is the real benediction. How often has some commonplace thing, some trouble or difficulty that others might call simply secular, become a link to bind us forever to His very throne, forming a chain of communication for infinite blessings. And, as a little bit of common glass is sufficient to reflect the full glory of the sun, so the smallest trifle has often had room in it for a whole heaven of God's love and help to come to us.

The trouble with Esau had vanished. The brothers met the next day with tears and embraces of affection from spirits that God had touched while Jacob prayed. Could you have seen behind the curtains that night, you would have beheld a sleepless man in his Idumean tent, tossing on his bed as he thinks of childhood's memories and fights with his bloody purpose of revenge. You might have said it was the impulse of a generous nature that made him spring to his feet and resolve that bygones should be bygones, and ride forth to meet that forgiven brother with the traces of tears still on his rugged face. No! No! It was God, it was prayer, it was the law of faith that binds unseen all hearts to the touch of His hand and the hands that touch His throne.

But this was the least part of it by far. Esau had

soon come and gone but Jacob's life moved forward still on that higher plane which began that night. From then on, he was God's Israel, fit to become the head of the chosen tribes.

How different God was to him after that experience—God was no longer at the distant top of the ladder, but near at hand, in his very embrace, and encompassing all his future life with His presence and blessing.

Dear friend, have you come to Peniel? Have you been left alone with Him who encompasses your path and your lying down? Have you received the touch that withers your thigh and slays your natural strength and confidence, and sends you forth a weak and halting man clothed with no power but God alone? Have you seen God face to face and had the throne of His presence brought down from heaven even unto your very heart? Blessed be God if it is so. Blessed even the trial that brought you to His feet and then to His face.

The Discipline of Trial

Jacob received his blessing. God then began to burn it into him in the crucible of suffering. We never know the full meaning of trial until we fully know the Lord. And so Jacob's severest trials came after his consecration. First was the dishonor of his daughter Dinah and the murder of the Shechemites by his willful sons, thus involving him in future strife with the inhabitants of the land. This was not so much a trial as a

punishment for his unjustifiable lingering on forbidden ground. God had sent him back to
Canaan, and he had no business tarrying.

We cannot remain upon the borders of an evil
world without real peril to us and our children.
Immediately after this came the command with
great and solemn emphasis: "Go up to Bethel and
settle there, and build an altar there to God"
(35:1). The house of God and the very gate of
heaven was henceforth to be his dwelling place.
And so renewing his consecration and separating
himself and his household from every doubtful
thing, he went back to the scene of his early
blessing, and reared at once the tent and the altar
to the God of Bethel.

It was well he did not wait, for the great and
bitter trials soon began which needed the refuge
and support of the divine presence.

His beloved Rachel was torn from his side in
the pangs of Benjamin's birth. Then Reuben
committed an unnatural crime and dishonored
his father's name in a way which on his dying bed
the old patriarch remembered with fatal emphasis. And then came the saddest, longest,
darkest, strangest trial of all—the loss of Joseph,
Rachel's firstborn son.

For a quarter of a century, perhaps, that weary
trial dragged along, and not one ray of light fell
on the blackness of his desolation. After that
came the years of famine, the necessity for the
journey to Egypt for corn, and the last drop in
the overflowing cup—the demand for little Ben-

jamin, too. It was too much for that broken heart to bear, and he cried out in agony: "Joseph is no more and Simeon is no more, and now you want to take Benjamin. Everything is against me" (42:36). But even this drop had to be drunk. All he had on earth he left in trust and complete abandonment in God's sole hands. And so he waited the issue.

It was enough. The cup was empty at last, and it was filled with a joy so strangely sweet that even Jacob's faith was scarcely able to believe it. To think that God could have for him after these buried years so great a joy—not only Benjamin safe, but Joseph too. It needed the sight of Joseph's wagons to convince him that it was true, and Jacob cried: "I'm convinced! My son Joseph is still alive" (45:28). Let us trust Him.

> It may be that the future
>   Will be less bitter than you think;
> Or if Marah must be Marah,
>   He will stand beside the brink,
> But it may be He is keeping
>   For the coming of your feet,
> Some gift of such rare blessedness,
>   Some joy so strangely sweet
> That your lips can scarcely utter
>   The thanks you cannot speak.

The Triumph

Jacob's triumph was marked by two characteristics. First, all evil was overruled by God's great hand, and out of the darkest providences Jacob saw blessing and honor come to his child, joy to his own heart, teaching to his wild and wayward sons, and salvation from famine for the whole world. He could truly say—instead of "Everything is against me" (42:36)—"The Angel who has delivered me from all harm—may he bless these boys" (48:16). Second, Jacob himself had learned to be still at last. The eager active spirit had quieted, and with a sense of all it meant he could say in his deathbed benediction: "I look for your deliverance, O LORD" (49:18). He had learned to wait. The restless heart was quieted at last and the "worm Jacob" was perfected through sufferings and able to ascend from the chrysalis of clay to the immortality of glory.

Out of filthy rags human skill loves to create wonders of the exquisite sheets that form our printed volumes, the illuminated card, the glowing picture, the letter of affection, the sacred Bible. Out of the soiled and wrecked remnants of human worthlessness God is making the tablets on which He loves to write His character, His thoughts and His own glorious image. Jacob glorified His exceeding and marvelous grace. So let us trust too; and in the ages to come He will "show the incomparable riches of his grace, expressed in his kindness to us in Christ Jesus" (Ephesians 2:7).

CHAPTER 7

Joseph

The Victory of Faith over Suffering and Wrong

By faith Joseph, when his end was near, spoke about the exodus of the Israelites from Egypt and gave instructions about his bones. (Hebrews 11:22)

The lesson of Joseph's life is the victory of faith over suffering and wrong. Jacob's sufferings were the discipline which his own waywardness brought upon him; Joseph's were the sufferings of an innocent and noble spirit. The former teach us how divine grace can overrule suffering for our spiritual good; the latter show how divine love can deliver us from the most trying difficulties and overrule them for our own good and the good of others.

Joseph's early visions were the foundation of his faith. He did not have, like Jacob, a divine prediction through his mother's lips, announcing his future life and place of covenant blessing. But to his

61

young heart there came in the visions of the night the foreshadowing of his future greatness, and, with ingenuous soul, he accepted it and believed it. His faith was tested by the ridicule of his brothers and even the grave surprise and questioning of his old father, but he kept it and confessed it, and the day came when he saw it all fulfilled.

A Word of Faith for the Future

To all who wait upon His will the Master gives some word of faith for the future. Today, not usually in dreams and visions, but in His Word and its bright illumination by the Spirit, does He draw aside the veil enough to give our faith a resting place and an anchorage. So to Timothy Paul speaks of "the prophecies once made about you, so that by following them you may fight the good fight" (1 Timothy 1:18). We must see the land before we can possess it.

It was this that carried David through his nine years of exile and persecution. It was this that sustained Paul through all his stormy vicissitudes: the will of God had said, you "must visit Rome" (Acts 19:21), and he counted not his life dear unto himself that he might "finish [his] course with joy" (20:24, KJV). And for each of us there is in life a destiny which God would have us claim and complete in faith and victory, and feel that if we trust Him He waits to carry us through.

"Lift up your eyes. . . . All the land that you see I will give to you" (Genesis 13:14-15).

The stern realities of life soon tested his ardent

anticipations and proved whether they were the dreams of an enthusiast or the faith of God. God will put our trust into the crucible, and all that is not founded on His will will dissolve like snow. But in that hour the faith of God shines with a luster more bright and clear because of the darkness and the trial.

The first trial was the cruel envy of his brethren and their heartless crime, which sent him into banishment and slavery and broke his father's heart with suspense and sorrow. Next came the base and false accusing of his mistress and his languishing in prison for months, and perhaps years. Finally he was neglected and deserted by his companion in bondage, whose deliverance he had foretold; as soon as he himself escaped, he left Joseph to his fate. Is there anything more cruel than a brother's disloyalty? Is there anything more bitter than envy? Has not the wisest of moralists said: "Who can stand before envy?" If there is anything still more hard to bear it is unjust accusation and inability to prove one's innocence under the charge of some atrocious crime. Such was Joseph's keen wound. It was pierced to the quick by the desertion, at the last, of the very friend he had tried to help in their common distress. Under such circumstances any one of us would have broken down completely, and said, perhaps, "there is no use trying. The more I attempt to do right the more I am hindered." Of course we are. The devil does not try to hinder people who are going down. The law of gravitation only works against you when you ascend; it helps you downward. So does the law of sin and death. But will we ask Satan's leave to be right and true and brave and victorious? Will we get a passport from him before we walk through the gates of victory? Or will we not rather count his fiercest challenge our best and most complimentary certificate, and say, "The highest evidence you can have that you are right is the devil's growl."

Reaction to Trials

How did Joseph act under trial? Did he get morbid, discouraged and mourn his hard fate? Did he wait until circumstances were favorable to do right and overcome? No; he at once accepted his position and made the best of it. He began to do his duty in the kitchen so faithfully that he soon became the foreman over all his master's house. Afterwards, when he was sent to prison, he did his work in prison so faithfully that he soon became the master of the situation and the over-seer of the prisoners.

The world is full of young men who are waiting for something worthy of them, and have no heart to do better because they are unfavorably situated. The man who is going to succeed on the throne must succeed first in the ranks. A young man came to me once, without work. He had been a bank officer. The next day he started out to mop out rail cars with a soap bucket and a brush. He did it well and gladly. He was thankful to have that to do and determined to do his best. It was not a week until

he was in a valuable clerkship in that railway company. Such men will succeed. God will bless brave,
manly, patient courage everywhere. Brother, begin
where you are.

There was no other road to Pharaoh's throne
except through that dungeon. Had Joseph not
been there amid the wrong and shame he could
not have been brought to the notice of the king as
he was and raised to his princely place. Instead of
quarreling with your trying position and blaming
someone for putting you there, why don't you
look for the side door that leads to the kingdom?
There is always such a door of faith for those who
trust God in all things. The secret of Joseph's victory was simply this: He believed that God was in
all this, even the bitterest of his trials, and would
carry him through and give him double for all his
shame. And I doubt not that often the memory of
his early visions came floating over his spirit to
point to the bright future which God was still
holding for him when the ordeal was past.

It came at last. It came directly through his
prison cell and his saddest experience. It came
with an uplift so glorious that his former troubles
were forgotten. With it came an opportunity for
the noblest revenge, for it not only laid the land
of Egypt at his feet, but it also brought his own
brothers to his feet to see the fulfillment of his
dreams and the failure of their envy, and to claim
at his hands the kindness which gave him his
crowning victory. Oh, yes, wronged and trusting
one, He hears your cries; He counts your tears.

God will lift up your head. He says of your enemies: "I will make them come and fall down at your feet and acknowledge that I have loved you" (Revelation 3:9). The pendulum must swing back with equal rebound. As we are partakers of His sufferings, so we shall be of His consolations.

> The Light of smiles shall fill again
>> The eyes that overflow with tears,
> And weary hours of grief and pain
>> Are harbingers of happier years.

God's Blessed "Afterward"

God's blessed "afterward" always comes. "No discipline seems pleasant at the time, but painful. Later on [afterward, KJV], however, it produces a harvest of righteousness and peace for those who have been trained by it" (Hebrews 12:11). Then the teardrops and blood-drops will be crystallized into pearls and rubies in our crowns. God has a wonderful way of balancing accounts. No true child of His need fear the touch of sorrow, for He can turn "the curse into a blessing" (Nehemiah 13:2); and overturn, when His time has come, the mightiest adversary; and turn the light affliction which was but for a moment into a far more exceeding and even eternal weight of glory. Like the contrary wind which the skillful sailor, by tacking, makes carry his vessel on its way, so "in all things God works for the good of those who love him" (Romans 8:28).

The best thing about Joseph's triumph was that

it was a victory of love. He did not use his exaltation for himself, but as a benefactor and savior of the world. His highest joy was to be able to return good for evil to the very brothers who had wronged him. It was not the joy of a mean revenge that filled his heart as he found the betrayers of his youth in his power, but it was the gladness of being able to do them a kindness. How noble was that kindness; how wisely did he endeavor to awake in their consciences a true sense of sin; and yet how generously did he try to rub out all sense of remorse and lead them to see in it all God's overruling love and power in bringing about their own deliverance as well as "the saving of many lives" (Genesis 50:20).

How can we have such love? What did the apostles say when Christ told them about the love that forgives until seventy times seven? "Increase our faith!" (Luke 17:5). Yes, it is only when we see God above all our trials that we can forgive and forget human instruments. Overruling and counteracting all their hate, we behold the hand of infinite power and love, and we fear them not; we only feel sorry for them, as we see their ultimate discomfiture and sorrow, and we can even love and bless those who curse us.

If we could ever see the hidden Hand that lies back of all other hands, we would ever have the victory of faith and love.

Is it not sublime to hear this wronged and outraged brother saying,

Do not be distressed and do not be angry with yourselves for selling me here, because it was to save lives that God sent me ahead of you. . . . But God sent me ahead of you to preserve for you a remnant on earth and to save your lives by a great deliverance.

So then, it was not you who sent me here, but God. He made me father to Pharaoh, lord of his entire household and ruler of all Egypt. (Genesis 45:5-8)

And then again, a little later, "You intended to harm me, but God intended it for good to accomplish what is now being done, the saving of many lives" (50:20).

That is faith's afterview of trial. It sees God's hand over all and recognizes no evil ultimately. To such a soul nothing can be amiss. Like Tauler's beggar, it can say:

Thou wishest me good morrow. I never had an ill morrow, for am I an hungered, I praise God; am I freezing, doth it hail, snow, rain, is it fair weather or foul, I praise God; and therefore had I never an ill morrow. Thou didst say, 'God prosper thee.' I have never been unprosperous, for I know how to live with God; I know that what He doth is best, and what God giveth or ordaineth for me, be it pain or pleasure, that I take cheerfully from Him as the best of all, and so I had never adversity. Thou wishest

God to bless me. I was never unblessed, for I desire to be only in the will of God, and I have so given up my will to the will of God, that what God willeth I will. Thou sayest: 'But what if His will should be to cast thee into hell? What wouldst thou do then?' Cast me into hell? His goodness holds Him back therefrom. Yet if He did, I should have two arms to embrace Him withal. One arm is true humility, and therewith am I one with His holy humanity. And with the right arm of love, that joineth His holy divinity, I would embrace Him so that he must come with me into hell likewise. And even so, I would sooner be in hell and have God, than in heaven and not have him.

Vision That Sees the Eternal

Joseph had not only looked over the span of life with victorious faith and hope, but his vision outreached the horizon of time and took in the eternal. His last words were as full of glorious expectation as his first. He "spoke about the exodus of the Israelites from Egypt and gave instructions about his bones" (Hebrews 11:22, see Genesis 50:24-26).

Yes, he saw in the distance their redemption, and a little further on the great redemption itself, and beyond that, the glorious resurrection. He claimed his place in that day with Abraham and Isaac and Jacob in the millennial earth and in the deathless, sinless, glorious kingdom of that greater Sufferer.

This Sufferer, like himself, was to be rejected and betrayed by His brethren, innocently accused and condemned, cruelly wronged, and then divinely exalted to be a Prince and a Savior, to deliver His people, to be made known to His long alienated brethren, and to be Ruler of all the families of the earth. Yes, it was fitting that Joseph should be the most beautiful and perfect type of Jesus. It was meet that this innocent and blameless life should point forward to Him who "committed no sin, and no deceit was found in his mouth" (1 Peter 2:22). It is satisfying that in this wronged and patient sufferer we should see His marred and bleeding face who was "despised and rejected by men, a man of sorrows, and familiar with suffering. . . . By oppression and judgment he was taken away" (Isaiah 53:3, 8), the face of One who "when they hurled their insults at him, . . . did not retaliate; when he suffered, he made no threats" (1 Peter 2:23). It is blessed to see in Joseph, that forgiving brother, the love that has thus sought and waited, and made Himself known to us. Forgiving us all, it has brought us to forgive ourselves and draw some good even from the lessons of our sinful past. And it is glorious to rise from Joseph's exaltation to Messiah's glory, and see Him reigning as a Prince and a Savior, not for Himself, but for His people's good, and saving and feeding a perishing world by His gracious hand.

It was He who lived and triumphed in Joseph, and "if we suffer, we shall also reign with him" (2 Timothy 2:12, KJV).

CHAPTER 8

Moses

Lessons from the Wilderness

*By faith Moses, when he had grown up,
refused to be known as the son of Pharaoh's
daughter. He chose to be mistreated along with
the people of God rather than to enjoy the
pleasures of sin for a short time. He regarded
disgrace for the sake of Christ as of greater
value than the treasures of Egypt, because he
was looking ahead to his reward. By faith he
left Egypt, not fearing the king's anger; he
persevered because he saw him who is invisible.
By faith he kept the Passover and the sprin-
kling of the blood, so that the destroyer of the
firstborn would not touch the firstborn of Israel. (Hebrews 11:24-28)*

In the development of the Holy Scriptures, the
Old Testament is preeminently a biography of
persons and the New Testament an exposition of
principles. The figures of the Old Testament illustrate the principles of the New and both

together constitute the abstract and concrete unfolding of sacred truth. Like a true teacher, God began with His infant children to teach by object lessons, and as they grew more mature, He led them into the deeper principles of His will. Therefore we find a far greater variety of character in the Old Testament than in the new, and yet all the characters illustrate the teachings of the Holy Spirit in the later records of inspiration. We need both records to complete the harmony of truth—like the famous window in the chapel of Oxford University, ornamented externally by Old Testament characters and internally by New Testament figures, so that when the sun shines through the colored glass it throws the blended figures upon the eye in an exquisite harmony of truth and beauty.

More than any other of the Old Testament characters Moses represents the typical idea. He himself has given us the most majestic series of gospel types which the Scriptures contain, and his own person was preeminently a figure of the Prophet who was to be raised up as he was. We may therefore expect, in the story of his life, to trace the highest and truest principles of spiritual teachings.

The Providential Framework

In every marked instrument which God employs for spiritual work, we may expect to see a cooperating providence preparing the way for the accomplishment of His will. In the case of Moses this providence was most signal. The very events which were intended by the adversary to destroy the people of God became the avenue through which deliverance came to Israel and destruction to Egypt. The decree which doomed the Hebrew children to death only opened the way for Moses to enter the house of Pharaoh and become the means for his destruction. Quite as marked was the divine hand which led his mother, first, to abandon him in the spirit of faith into the arms of God and then to see him brought back, without her moving a finger, so that she became the instructor of his childhood in the palace of the queen. Thus God adjusts His plan to the circumstances of our lives, to teach us that, instead of deploring our difficult situations and giving up in despair, we can expect Him to use them like Joseph's prison and Moses' cradle as the very steppingstones to our highest usefulness.

His Education and Preparation

The spiritual advantages enjoyed by Moses in the house of Pharaoh were part of the divine plan for his future usefulness. "Educated in all the wisdom of the Egyptians" (Acts 7:22), he was able to meet on equal terms the proud priesthood and arrogant Pharaoh, and also to show to future ages the infinite superiority of the wisdom of God to all the intellectual achievements of the world. In his marvelous system of legislation there is no trace anywhere of his having copied the precedents of the past or adopted anything even from

Egyptian civilization. His whole system is divinely original. Standing on the very heights of human progress he rejects it all, and receives directly from heaven the law of righteousness and the light of truth. No doubt, however, his broad culture enlarged the vessel which God was so wonderfully to fill and use. Still it is true that God can use and even does choose the most cultivated minds and the most accomplished instruments to fulfill His highest work.

Better far, however, than all the wisdom of Egypt, was his mother's holy teaching. From her he drank in the story of the past—the calling of Abraham, the covenants with Isaac and Jacob, the faith of Joseph, the wrongs of the Hebrews, the providences of his birth and childhood—until his very blood was saturated with that spirit of heroic loyalty and of devotion to his people and his God, which all the allurements of the world were not able to counterbalance. We know something of the spirit of his teacher by the story of her maternal faith and consecration. A mother who could so commit her baby to the arms of Providence and receive him back, like Isaac, as from the dead, could not possibly fail to transcribe her own lofty character and faith upon the heart of the child that was so wholly committed to her influence and teaching. We will have to wait for eternity to know how much of the grandeur of Moses' life was but the reflection of Jochabed's own character.

The Choice of Moses

The crisis of his life came at length. Not always can we lie on the pillow of a mother's faithful breast and be supported by her faith and love. The hour comes when all men and women must choose for themselves and prove the strength of their convictions by the divine purpose of their life. That hour found Moses uncompromisingly prepared "rather than to enjoy the pleasures of sin for a short time. He regarded disgrace for the sake of Christ as of greater value than the treasures of Egypt" (Hebrews 11:25-26).

This choice was not easily made. It involved the distinct renunciation by him of his assumed place as the son of Pharaoh's daughter and required that he should sacrifice all the honors and prospects involved in this claim, as well as incur, perhaps, her bitter displeasure by his acknowledgment. But he took the full responsibility and stepped out into reproach and peril as a true confession of the God of Israel and a fellow-sufferer with his despised and doomed race. God can use only natures that are uncompromising in their devotion to Him. True-hearted loyalty and singleness of purpose are essential to greatness of character or effectiveness in service. From the beginning Moses was unequivocally on the Lord's side. Let his example speak to a time-serving generation and reecho the Master's message, "You cannot serve both God and Money" (Matthew 6:24). Do not wait until you have tasted the cup of pleasure and sated the passions of youth and have only the dregs of life to give to God. But when the brimming cup is within your reach and all that earth can offer may be yours by a course of decent moderation and simply walking round the Master's cross a little, then it is that God appreciates and gloriously recompenses the spirit that can unhesitatingly dash it from our lips and commit ourselves to our Master's cause and our Master's cross with all it may involve.

A lovely girl, the daughter of a proud English family, had given her heart to Christ. Her father, a man of the world, was bitterly disappointed, especially when he found her religious principles were going to separate her altogether from his worldly pursuits and pleasures. Earnestly he pleaded with her to attend one party more and sing with her superb voice to entertain his fashionable friends. At length she yielded, and while a strange hush fell upon all the brilliant company, she allowed him to lead her to the piano. Sitting down she touched the keys, and looking into the faces of her friends, while tears burst from her eyes, she sang as never before,

> Jesus, I my cross have taken,
> All to leave and follow Thee,
> Let the world despise, forsake me,
> They have scorned my Savior too.

The notes were lost in the sobs of many voices. But for her the blessing was beyond all that they

received; it had committed her forever to the un-
reserved confession of Christ. If we are going to
separate ourselves unto Christ, the more
thoroughly we do it the easier it will be in the
end. One bold fearless plunge and we will find
ourselves on the ground of entire consecration
where alone we will be able to stand.

Moses' First Service and Failure

Like his people afterwards and like many a
Christian life, Moses had to fail before he could
finally succeed. Every true life has a grave behind
it, when in lowly and painful crucifixion the
strength and confidence of nature were exchanged for the strength of God. And so Moses
stepped forth in the strength of his impulsive enthusiasm to deliver his people. Seeing a Hebrew
brother suffering wrong, he sprang to his rescue
and slew his assailant, and buried his body in the
sand. He had imagined that his people would at
once hail him as their deliverer. But when he
found that his rash act was known and that even
his own people were likely to prove his betrayers,
his great purpose sank in reaction and despair,
and he fled from Egypt to the desert of Midian.
His beautiful dream was shattered. It was the ef-
fervescence of human impulse, and it never could
have stood the tests of the struggle. When he
returned to the conflict later, he was a timid, self-
depreciating man, his confidence and impetuous-
ness gone. He was a thousandfold more fitted for
his mighty work with the strength of Jehovah

than with the impulsive fiery spirit of 40 years before.

So Moses in the Old Testament, Simon Peter in the New, and all the honored servants of God must learn the two secrets of service: *self-insufficiency*, God's *all-sufficiency*. Then when self is in the dust God can work effectually.

The symbol of Moses' power, when God at length did send him forth, was a little rod. It was not a jeweled scepter that God used to break the power of Egypt, but a plain little rod cut from the thorn bushes of the desert—a symbol of Moses himself.

Moses' Deeper Spiritual Preparation for His Work

Few men ever had such a schooling as the great Lawgiver. First, for 40 years, he had all the advantages of earthly culture and then for 40 years more he dwelt with God alone in the solitudes of Midian. Doubtless this was the best of all his classes in the school of God. At first it may have seemed that the years were lost in inactivity and vanity, and that his life was wearing away beside his sheepfolds and amid his dusky family. As the decades slowly rolled on he found himself 40, 50 and at last 60 years of age with nothing accomplished. The winter of age was already marking his head with its warnings of life's close, and perhaps he had already learned these stanzas of his sublime poem,

We finish our years with a moan.
The length of our days is seventy years—
    or eighty, if we have the strength;
yet their span is but trouble and sorrrow,
    for they quickly pass, and we fly away.
(Psalm 90:9-10)

So he may have been singing in sorrowful strains during the last decade of his life in Midian and thinking that his span was almost ended and his work not yet begun.

Such an experience some of us may know, but these years, as we have already found are not wasted but are the very soil of life's future harvests and the time of education for life's noblest work. Let us not be weary if the time seems long and the lesson slow. There are some things which must be burned into the soul by years rather than days of quiet reflection and long communion with God and our own hearts. Calmly and thoroughly were the lessons learned under the shadows of Horeb and amid the oasis of the desert, and when the years of action came, Moses found that not one moment had been lost. During all those years his heart remained true to his people and his purpose. One little token expresses the story of years. It was the name he gave his child, born to him in the years of exile. He did not settle down in his new household with forgetful contentment and abandon the memories of the past and the hopes of the future. When Gershom, his firstborn, looked up into his face and smiled, Moses dropped a tear, heaved a sigh even in his new joy, and expressed in his baby's name the thought that was deep in his heart—"an alien in a foreign land" (Exodus 2:22).

So let us hold fast amid life's wearing years and the trials which seem to contradict our bright promises, to the faith and hope and love that anchor us to God and our life purpose. Let us not despise the time of education nor weary of the long lessons of God's providence, "for at the proper time we will reap a harvest if we do not give up" (Galatians 6:9).

It was from the wilderness of Gilead that Elijah came to startle the centuries with his bold and mighty voice; it was from the deserts of Arabia that Paul returned to give the Gentile nations the gospel; it was from the quiet years of Nazareth and the carpenter's bench that Jesus went forth to the ministry from which all other ministries flow; and still God teaches His servants, in the school of silence, separation and communion with Himself, the secret of their life work.

Moses' Life Work

As a man of 80, ready it would seem to natural reason to drop into the grave, the work of his life began and for nearly half a century he went forth to a career of unparalleled activity and usefulness. It would take long to even enumerate the labors of his life. First, he was the founder of a nation and led the greatest movement of history through the most critical years of its existence. He found a race of slaves with scarcely spirit enough to accept their freedom and he left them a victorious nation on the threshold of the fairest of earth's inheritances.

Second, he was the legislator not only of his nation but of all time. The principles of morality which he inculcated are the basis of all true ethics, and the ideas which he gave to the world were the source of all the light that has followed, of which even the philosophy of ancient sages was but the dim reflection.

Third, he was the great historian of the past, and all we know of earth's first 25 centuries is from his pen.

Fourth, he was the great prophet of the future, the revealer of the gospel age which he was but anticipating in his marvelous types and ceremonial institutions.

Fifth, we may call him the founder of the Holy Scriptures. The first five books of our Bible are from Moses' pen, and his name is forever inscribed on the very pillars of inspiration. And all the shallow criticisms of modern rationalism will never be able to efface the record or dishonor the enduring monument of his life and work. Such a work after the ordinary period of life was finished, stands unrivaled in the records of time, and, like the marble statue of Michelangelo or the towering peaks of his own Mount Sinai, leaves his colossal figure, sublime, supreme among the clouds and the stars.

Moses' Character

After the experience of Midian, we expect to find a new man. We are not disappointed. The work we have just described could not have been accomplished by the old Moses.

His predominant feature is henceforth humility. As slow to step to the front as he had been rash, and with excessive timidity which God had to reprove, he answered, "Who am I, that I should go to Pharaoh and bring the Israelites out of Egypt" (Exodus 3:11). God's answer was sufficient: "I will be with you" (3:12). There was no need for Moses to be anything, for God was to be everything. The only "I" henceforth that was of any consequence was the "I AM WHO I AM" (3:14). This is the indispensable qualification for power and service in every life.

Abreast of this was a faith which took hold of God in proportion as it let go of self. From this time he ventured not only his own fortunes, but the fortunes of a nation, on the naked arm of Jehovah, and became one ceaseless miracle of providence and power.

The spirit of love, meekness and long-suffering formed the crowning glory of this surpassing character. The Holy Scriptures have declared that Moses was the meekest of men. His sublime self-sacrifice in throwing himself between his offending people and the impending justice of God, "Please forgive their sin—but if not, then blot me out of the book you have written" (32:32), has no equal except Christ's prayer for His murderers and His intercession for sinful men. His unwearied endurance of the provocation and rebellion that burdened all his life and not only kept them, but even himself out of Canaan, reached the very heights of the love that "always protects, always trusts, always hopes, always perseveres" (1 Corinthians 13:7).

His godliness completed the features of this heavenly character. Beyond all other men, even of the Old Testament, he knew Jehovah and lived in His intimate fellowship. He talked to God, face to face, as a man with his friend. He dwelt with God for 40 days in His inaccessible glory until his face shone with an immortal radiance which the mortal eye dare not behold. He died in His bosom and was buried by His hand alone. Truly his prayer was answered, "Show me your glory" (Exodus 33:18).

But his life and character were not without their faults and failures. And the failure was in the strongest, not the weakest part. The meekest of men was the one who lost his patience. The ages must learn through Moses the insufficiency of the best of men, and the need of something better than the law to give the secret of perfect victory. The secret of Moses' failures was this: "The law made nothing perfect, but the bringing in of a better hope *did*" (Hebrews 7:19, KJV). And this was why his life work also came short of full realization. He saw but did not enter the Promised Land. The founder of the Law had to be its victim, that his life and death might demonstrate the inability of the Law to lead any man into the Promised Land. The very fact that it was for so slight a fault that Moses lost his inheritance makes all the more emphatic the solemn sentence of the law. "Cursed is everyone who does not continue to do everything written in the Book of the Law" (Galatians 3:10).

But to the glory of the grace of God we can add that what the Law could not do for Moses the gospel did; and he who could not pass over Jordan under the old dispensation was seen on the very heights of Hermon with the Son of Man, sharing His transfiguration glory, and talking of that death on Calvary to which he owed his glorious destiny.

That grace we have inherited under the gospel of Jesus Christ. Let its mighty privileges and promises inspire us to a faith, a holiness and a consecration such as Moses could not know. From Sinai and Pisgah let us pass with the Captain of our salvation to Calvary and Hermon, and prove all the fullness of His uttermost salvation.

CHAPTER 9

Joshua

Lessons in the Good Fight of Faith

By faith the walls of Jericho fell, after the people had marched around them for seven days. (Hebrews 11:30)

The fact that Joshua alone of the Old Testament worthies bears the very name of Jesus and is the special type of the "Captain of our Salvation," would prepare our minds to expect in his life and characters the most marked and impressive qualities. His work bears the same relation to that of Moses that the gospel does to the law, and faith to human effort. We may therefore look for the very highest lessons of faith in the story of his life, which might indeed be called in the language of the New Testament, "the good fight of faith" (1 Timothy 6:12). But faith has its roots as well as its fruits, and Joshua's triumphs began far back in the discipline of the wilderness.

Joshua as a Servant

He is introduced to us as the servant of Moses, or more literally, "Joshua, . . . Moses' aide" (Joshua 1:1). The first qualification of leadership is to have learned to follow and obey. The best generals have come from the ranks. Moses' successor was for 40 years Moses' servant. Joshua's submission to Moses expressed a good deal more than service to an earthly master. It really implied his submission to the law and that deeper spiritual discipline, which must come in every successful life, in the surrender of self and the complete subjection of self-will to the perfect will of God. Joshua's greater successor and antitype, the Lord Jesus Christ, was "born under law, to redeem those under law, that we might receive the full rights of sons" (Galatians 4:4-5). The law has its indispensable place in the discipline of every Christian life, and the more thorough the work, the more complete will our sanctification be. If we, like Joshua, have had our full apprenticeship in the service of Moses, we can say, "For through the law I died to the law so that I might live for God" (2:19).

Joshua and Amalek

It is not a mere accident that we find Joshua leading the hosts of Israel in their first battle with Amalek in the wilderness. Amalek, we know, was the type of the flesh, and Joshua's victory represents the conflict with our old and carnal self.

Not only must we learn to bow to the law, but we must learn to trample the flesh under our feet. Every victor must first be a self-conqueror. But the method of Joshua's victory was the uplifted arm of Moses on the Mount. As he held up his hands Joshua prevailed; as he lowered them Amalek prevailed. It was to be a battle of faith, not of human strength, and the banner that was to wave over the discomfited foe, "Jehovah-nissi." This too is the secret of our spiritual triumph. If we are led of the Spirit, we will not fulfill the lusts of the flesh. "Sin shall not be your master, because you are not under law, but under grace" (Romans 6:14). Have we thus begun the battle and in the strength of Christ planted our feet on our own necks, and thus victorious over the enemy in the citadel of the heart, been set at liberty for the battle of the Lord and the service of others? It was the lack of this that hindered the life of Saul and it has wrecked many promising careers. One enemy in the heart is stronger than 10,000 in the field. May the Lord lead us all into Joshua's first triumph, and show us the secret of self-crucifixion through that greater Joshua who alone can lead us on to holiness and victory!

Joshua as a Faithful Witness for God

The time soon came when Joshua had to take a more positive stand in the line of that life of faith to which he was divinely called, and show that he could trust his Lord in the face of difficulty and in the midst of opposition. He was appointed as one of the spies to search out the land. On his return with his brethren the crisis of his life occurred. We know the story of the spies' ignoble fear and cowardly faithlessness. It was then that he and Caleb stood true to God and nobly declared in the face of a rebellious and mutinous multitude that the task to which God had called them was not too hard, and that if they would but trust and obey and be true to God, He would bring them into their inheritance, and their enemies would find their strength departed from them. It was a forlorn hope which he so bravely led, but nonetheless he stood true to his post and won his future recompense.

It is not our success in witnessing for God that counts, but our fidelity. Caleb and Joshua were grandly faithful and God remembered it when the day of visitation came. It was a very difficult and unpopular position, and all of us are called in the crisis of our lives to stand alone. In this very matter of trusting God for victory over sin and our full inheritance in Christ we have all to be tested very much as Joshua was. Our brethren even in the Church of God, while admitting in the abstract the loveliness and advantages of such an ideal life, tell us as they told Israel that it is impractical and impossible, and many of us have to stand alone for years witnessing to the power of Christ to save His people to the uttermost. But this is the real victory of faith and the proof of our uncompromising fidelity. It is men who have learned to stand where Joshua stood whom God can trust with the great interests of His kingdom in the hour of peril. Let us not therefore complain when we suffer reproach for our testimony or stand alone for God, but thank Him that He so honors us, and so stand the test that He can afterwards use us when the multitudes are glad to follow.

Joshua's Waiting Years

He too, like Moses, had to go through the wilderness. He had chosen the Lord uncompromisingly and his inheritance was assured, but he had to wait for 40 years until the unbelieving generation had passed away and the fullness of the time had come. So faith with us all must be tested by the hardest of all ordeals, waiting. This little word runs like a silver thread through all the promises. "Wait for the LORD; be strong and take heart and wait for the LORD" (Psalm 27:14).

It is not as hard to give one testimony for God even in the face of peril and the prospect of death, as to stand immoveable in the attitude of faith through all the years of disappointment and delay while all the influences around us are fitted to depress and hinder. There was very little in that half century of ceaseless tramping through the desert amid a gainsaying people to sustain the faith of Joshua. The time seemed to be wasted and the precious years to be going by in vain and he to be suffering for the sake of a worthless multitude who did not even appreciate his forbearance and patience. But all this discipline served to ripen his character, as the long summer days mellow the rich fruit of autumn. Horticulturists tell us that the autumn apples are much richer and more durable than the early fruit of summer. It is because they have had the summer heat and the slow maturity of the whole season. So the great Husbandman honored the faith of Joshua, and so He is teaching us in the school of patience the lesson which could not be learned in a moment of impatience or an outburst of impulsive haste. Let us be patient. Let us learn to wait. Let us accept the long lessons and the slow developments of His providence and grace, and we will find as He had said, "They shall not be ashamed that wait for me" (Isaiah 49:23, KJV), and that our blessings like good investments carry compound interest and multiply as they linger.

Joshua's Life Work

At last in the maturity of his years the high calling came and the mantle of Moses fell upon his servant, and even a higher ministry than he had claimed opened before the well-trained soldier. The work to which he was called was that of a soldier, to lead his people into their inheritance and subdue their enemies before them. The charge given to him in the first chapter of Joshua reveals thus both the nature of his commission and the secret of his success. Two watchwords stand prominent: faith and obedience. "Be strong and very courageous" (Joshua 1:7) was the first condition of victory, and the second, "Be careful to obey all the law my servant Moses gave you; do not turn from it to the right or to the left" (1:7). Armed with these two charges he went forward to a career of conquest, unexampled in the history of war: first, subjecting in three great campaigns no less than 31 sovereignties; and then dividing their inheritance among his followers, and thus laying the foundation of the future state according to the direction of Jehovah on an equitable and permanent foundation. If Moses was the greatest of legislators, Joshua was the greatest of conquerors and administrators. And yet the work was not his own, for he was but the echo of another voice and the instrument of a mightier hand. The very secret of his life lay wholly in the fact that it was entirely a life and work of faith, and he himself but the obedient instrument of the greater Captain who went before him. For this, after all, is the essence of faith, to let God work and to be simply the responsive instrument of His power and will. This was Joshua's work, and so God worked in him mightily "to demolish strongholds" (2 Corinthians 10:4) and the building up of His kingdom.

The Characteristics of Joshua

He was preeminently a man of action. Few of his speeches are recorded and even they sound like deeds rather than words. The commission given to him says nothing about what he should say but only about the places where he should set the soles of his feet. This was to be the feature of his life work, putting his feet down on

God's commands and promises and marching on in victory. He was not only a man of action but of very forceful and positive action. When he put his foot down it meant something. He put his whole weight on it; the whole force of his being was in all he did. Nowhere in the history of war is there anything to be compared for strength and celerity of movement and stroke with the battle of Gibeon, where, marching all night, he suddenly threw himself like an avalanche on the confederate kings and broke their ranks to pieces by the tremendous power of the blow.

Joshua was also a man of persevering action; the enterprise that he began he thoroughly completed. When he started to march around Jericho he never stopped until the seventh round on the seventh day was completed and the walls had fallen with a crash of thunder. When he fell like a thunderbolt on the hosts of the Canaanites at Beth Horon he never stopped until they were utterly destroyed. And when the day itself was too short, he lifted his hand to heaven and stayed the sun and moon until the work was finished. When he began the work of conquering Canaan he ceased only when it could be written, "So Joshua took the entire land" (Joshua 11:23). Beloved, what are we doing to act our faith, and how fully are we finishing our work?

Joshua's Failures

These qualities were not without their human imperfections; but even these are encouraging, as they teach us how God can overcome even our mistakes and bring good out of our shortcomings.

The first failure was through the sin of Achan. But when this was thoroughly put away in judgment, it was overruled for greater good and Israel went forward in uninterrupted victory. Another failure for which Joshua was more directly responsible was the haste and impulsiveness with which he yielded to the request of the Gibeonites and allowed them to ensnare him into a forbidden alliance, thus entangling all the future by a league which was directly contrary to the command of God. Yet doubtless this also taught valuable lessons and more watchful dependence upon God for counsel and direction in every step and prevented future complications.

These imperfections teach us that in the most advanced Christian life we are not ever a moment safe without entire dependence upon the wisdom and power of God, and the more terrible declension, which followed the death of Joshua and left Israel before long in a worse condition than even the wilderness, only shows the more emphatically how the most consecrated life needs to watch against temptation and walk closely with the Master. The closing years of Joshua's life were spent in serenity and rest in the city which Israel gave him as an inheritance. Its very name, Timnath Serah, is finely expressive of the blessing which follows a victorious life of faith. It means "the City of the Sun," and suggests the fullness of light and divine guidance and communion which God will recompense both here and hereafter to those who fight the good fight of faith. Of such He had said, "God is not ashamed to be called their God, for he has prepared a city for them" (Hebrews 11:16). And even here they walk in the light of that city which "does not need the sun . . . for the glory of God gives it light, and the Lamb is its lamp" (Revelation 21:23). For he who walks with God in obedient faith "will dwell on the heights, whose refuge will be the mountain fortress. . . . Your eyes will see the king in his beauty and view a land that stretches afar" (Isaiah 33:16-17). There is a place of rest and fellowship where we may dwell with God in light and cloudless communion above the scenes of earthly strife and sin. Come beloved, and "let us walk in the light of the LORD" (2:5).

The best of all the lessons of this victorious career is that which leads us to a better Captain, to lose sight of Joshua as we look unto Jesus, "the author and perfecter of our faith" (Hebrews 12:2) who not only has set for us the pattern of obedience, but who comes to take us by the hand and lead us to the heights of victory. The most instructive scene in Joshua's life was where, prostrate on his face before the walls of Jericho, he ceased to be captain and accepted the leadership of the heavenly Master, who stood above him exclaiming, "Take off your sandals" (Joshua 5:15); "as commander of the army of the LORD have I now come" (5:14). From that hour Joshua was himself but a follower, and a form unseen marched before him, while he constantly asked, "What message does my Lord have for his servant?" (5:14).

This is the attitude of victory for us all; Joshua has passed away but Jesus remains "the same yesterday and today and forever" (Hebrews 13:8).

> Our Captain calls us forth,
> To conquest and a crown;
> Our feet, through Him, shall tread
> The powers of darkness down,
> A feeble saint shall win the day,
> Though death and hell obstruct the way.

CHAPTER 10

Caleb

Lessons in Faithfulness

Then Joshua blessed Caleb, son of Jephunneh and gave him Hebron as his inheritance. So Hebron has belonged to Caleb son of Jephunneh the Kenizzite ever since, because he followed the LORD, the God of Israel, wholeheartedly. (Joshua 14:13-14)

The word Caleb signifies a "dog." There is no finer pattern of humble faithfulness. The preeminent characteristic of Caleb was that he followed the Lord fully.

His Faith

Faithfulness always begins in faith. The faith of Caleb is clearly implied in the promise referred to in his appeal to Joshua (14:6-12) to give him Hebron for his inheritance. He claimed it because it was the land his own feet had walked on 45 years before. The treading of his feet on Hebron was a very significant act. To do so he had to press through the perils of a hostile land and to venture within the walls of the mightiest of all the fortified cities of Canaan. Hebron was the oldest and most formidable stronghold of the giant nations of the land, and yet Caleb dared as a friendless spy to enter their borders alone and plant his feet on the frowning battlements. When he did so, there went up from his heart the first longing cry that God would yet give him the place as his own inheritance.

There are moments in all our lives when the promise of the future is born of a faith and hope which are but dimly understood—when in some hour of high and holy aspiration the keener vision of the spirit seems to penetrate beyond the curtains of the present and we catch a glimpse of God's yet unrevealed purpose for us. Like the dreams of Joseph, we anticipate something of that good and perfect will of God which later years are to bring, and claim the inheritance which may yet lie far in the distance.

This, no doubt, was the spirit in which Caleb set his feet on the heights of Hebron. God would have us first believe His great promises and then wait and trust through the testing years, and then in the happy future look back and praise His faithfulness. Perhaps there is nothing in the future inheritance of the heavenly world which the Lord would not have us anticipate and believe for, even in the present. Life is not bounded by the narrow horizon of time. There are still greater hopes that take hold of the ages to come, and many times the sun that goes down upon dis-appointed expectations will rise beyond in more glorious fulfillment, and no heart that has sweetly trusted the fullness of God will ever be disap-pointed.

So God let Jacob wait through the dark years during which he saw not, but at last the answer came and he went home with the grateful cry: "I have waited for thy salvation, O LORD" (Genesis 49:18, KJV). So for years, He held before the heart of David his crown and kingdom, while every outward appearance contradicted the hope. Faith saw the day when it could say to other weary pilgrims, "I had fainted, unless I had believed to see the goodness of the LORD in the land of the living. Wait on the LORD: be of good courage, and he shall strengthen thine heart" (Psalm 27:13-14, KJV).

But the day came when the faith which had claimed the inheritance on Hebron's heights received the promise from Moses' lips in the dark hour of Israel's rebellion. "The land on which your feet have walked will be your inheritance" (Joshua 14:9). Henceforth faith had a divine word of unfailing promise to depend on, and to that word it clung in unfaltering confidence through all the years of the wilderness. This is the sure resting place of faith, and when God once gives us His word let us never even allow a shadow of doubt to fall upon the confidence of our faith.

Are we thus walking by faith? Have we anchored our future to the Word of God, for our salvation, for our spiritual experience, for our needs, for our hopes of service, for the giant difficulties of life, for the holy desires which He had put on our hearts, for the friends who are more to us than our own lives? Do we have His Word for it and are we clinging to it as Caleb to his promise? On such a soul all heaven looks down and God cannot disappoint it.

Caleb's Faithfulness

It is not enough to trust God for ourselves, but we must confess Him before His enemies. Our faith has to be acknowledged and His faithfulness vindicated and honored before an unbelieving world. Have you ever noticed how much the services which the Scriptures record in the lives of all the saints are mainly of this character? We are not told how much they did or said, so much as that they were witnesses for God and bore faithful testimony to Him in the face of His enemies and in the midst of abounding unbelief. The whole of the 11th chapter of Hebrews, the biography of the Old Testament saints and heroes, is just a list of personal testimonies, and all these men and women are called witnesses. The one business of each of their lives was to bear witness of God. What was Noah's life but a consistent witness-bearing to one of God's messages? What was Abraham's life but a consistent testifying for God as true and faithful? And what is the name that Christ gives to us in our services for Him but that of witnesses for Him?

Caleb was called to be a witness in an hour when his people doubted and feared. Then he stood boldly forward and declared that God was faithful and able to fulfill His promises.

And so each of us is called to be a witness of God's faithfulness. Our salvation is not chiefly for our own sake, but as Paul says, "For that very reason I was shown mercy so that in me, the worst of sinners, Christ Jesus might display his unlimited patience as an example for those who would believe on him and receive eternal life" (1 Timothy 1:16).

The reason He sanctifies us is that we may witness to others of His power to save to the uttermost. He delivers us that we may show forth His salvation to the world. He heals us that we may go home to our friends and tell them what great things the Lord has done for us. He answers prayer that the blessing received may be a testimony to encourage others to trust Him.

When George Mueller began to ask God for the means to build his orphanage, he declared that it was not so much to relieve the distress as to prove to the world the faithfulness of God in answering the prayers of His people. Each of us in our place has abundant opportunity, and especially in the hardest places, to be witnesses for Him. Of every situation in which we can be placed it may be true as He said of His disciples, even when brought before councils, "This will result in your being witnesses to them" (Luke 21:13). Have we thus accepted our life as an opportunity in which to glorify Him, and in the face of difficulty and un-belief, are we wholly following the Lord our God?

Caleb's Long Trial

The faith and the faithfulness were at length brought to the test of years. That is very much harder than the brief ordeal through which he had passed in the day of his faithful testimony. He had to wait nearly half a century, holding fast to his purpose and his promise, while all around him there was nothing but discouragement and despair, and every minute brought the dying groan of some sinking comrade.

It is the long discipline of delay that puts the test to the hearts of God's children, but it is this also that matures it and multiplies the blessing as it comes. The blossom of the century plant comes slowly, but it is a royal flower when it bursts its lingering petals. Man's redemption waited 40 cen-turies before it came, but millions of years will not suffice to unfold its accumulated grace and glory.

> Let us not become weary in doing good, for at the proper time we will reap a harvest if we do not give up. (Galatians 6:9)
>
> You need to persevere so that when you have done the will of God, you will receive what he has promised. (Hebrews 10:36)
>
> So do not throw away your confidence; it will be richly rewarded. (10:35)

Caleb's Recompense

At length it came. He was 85 when the promise reached its harvest. But remember that Moses was 80 when he began his great life work, and Joshua 86. In God's great element life is not counted by years but by the measure of life which He imparts. There is no need that we should give up in imbecility because the course of nature seems exhausted. There are divine resources which can quicken the aged pulse and renew our youth like the eagle's.

The first element in Caleb's reward was the marvelous physical strength which God imparted to him because he wholly followed the Lord his God. Standing erect without a faltering nerve, he cried with his gray locks streaming in the air, "Now then, just as the LORD promised, he has kept me alive for forty-five years . . . So here I am today, eighty-five years old! I am still as strong today as the day Moses sent me out; I'm just as vigorous to go out to battle now as I was then" (Joshua 14:10-11). It was not natural vigor but supernatural life. The others fell because of disobedience, but he was preserved because of his fidelity.

The covenant which God had made when they came forth from Egypt was that if they would diligently hearken to His voice and keep His statues, He would be their Healer and Keeper, and to Joshua and Caleb it was gloriously and literally fulfilled. He will still keep the feet of His faithful saints who wholly follow the Lord their God. It may not be until we are Caleb's age, but it will surely be before our life work is accomplished.

The promise of God was literally fulfilled, and Hebron was given to Caleb as his inheritance. The very word of God came to pass without abatement or compromise, and in kind; just what had been promised was literally fulfilled, and his feet were permitted to tread the heights of Hebron, and his life to close in the city of Abraham and David with the blessed consciousness that not a single expectation had been disappointed. How sweet the fulfillment of promises which look back over half a century of waiting and weeping hours! How delightful in life's eventide to recall the hopes of youth and to trace the steps by which God's faithful providence has led us without a single failure on His part into our full inheritance!

But Caleb's promise must be claimed at last by the same courageous faith which had believed for it in the beginning. When the hour of fulfillment came it did not drop into his life unasked or unrecognized; it had to be specifically claimed and bravely won in the strength of God. Perhaps he might have missed his blessing if he had been discouraged or indifferent, but he bravely stepped forward, claimed it and gloriously played the soldier and the man in the good fight of faith, looking undismayed on the mighty Anakites and saying, "The LORD helping me, I will drive them out just as he said" (14:12).

Do we not sometimes fail just here? Are there not promises waiting for us to claim a land into which we are to step and find that every place that the sole of our foot will tread upon the Lord has given us? God's promises must be taken as well as given, entered upon by the feet of victorious faith if they would be fully realized. God is always there by His presence and power to enable us to claim them in all their fullness. There is no height of difficulty or battlement of hostile foes which we will dare to claim in His strength, but He is ready to support us and make us more than conquerors.

The achievement of Caleb had a deep spiritual meaning beyond the ordinary lessons of faith. The name Hebron means "the friend," and was a symbol of that higher relationship with God which we enter when we overcome in the battle of faith. For each of us there is a Hebron too, a place of fellowship over which God has inscribed for us the inspiring words, "He who overcomes will inherit all this, and I will be his God and he will be my son" (Revelation 21:7).

And so we read in the closing verse of the chapter that after Caleb's victory the land had rest from war. There is a peace which comes from war, and a rest which we will never know until we dare to face the hardest foe and overcome the very citadel of our enemy. There are places in every one of our lives as difficult as Hebron to Caleb. These are the very places which God afterwards crowns with the glory of His presence.

Finally, this beautiful incident teaches us that there are high achievements and demands awaiting God's children, even after they have reached what would ordinarily be called a very high spiritual experience. Caleb had already come out of the wilderness and crossed the Jordan. Already he had been for five years in the land of promise and had joined in the battles which had overcome the 31 kings of Canaan. Surely that was achievement enough for a lifetime! But no, he counted his work but scarcely begun, and after all that he stepped out into the most glorious victory of his life. Let his example incite us who have known much of the Master's faithfulness to hear:

> God's all-animating voice
> That calls thee from on high,
> 'Tis His own hand presents the prize
> To thine aspiring eye.
>
> A cloud of witnesses around,
> Hold thee in full survey;
> Forget the steps already trod,
> And onward urge thy way.

CHAPTER 11

Gideon

The Strength of Weakness

The LORD turned to him and said, "Go in the strength you have and save Israel out of Midian's hand. Am I not sending you?"

"But Lord," Gideon asked, "how can I save Israel? My clan is the weakest in Manasseh, and I am the least in my family."

The LORD answered, "I will be with you."
(Judges 6:14-16)

A nation's most illustrious characters are developed through times of trouble. The heroes of the past have been brought to light, like precious gems torn from the heart of the mountain, by the earthquakes and convulsions that upheaved society. This is especially true of the loftiest characters of the Bible. They shine like stars in the firmament of night. It was in the darkest hour of the world, when there was but one saint in all earth's population, that Noah lived his life of separation and testimony; it was in the very midnight of his people's history that Moses came forth; it was when Israel was rushing wildly to the very precipice of ruin that Elijah appeared, and by his ministry of fire, lighted up for a little the deepening gloom and checked the hastening catastrophe; and it was in the dark period of the judges that many of the most striking figures of Old Testament biography were brought to light.

Of these, perhaps the most striking is Gideon, and the lesson of his life is as clear as the point of the diamond. Expressed in a single phrase it is the "strength of weakness" and might all be clustered around one passage in First Corinthians:

> God chose the foolish things of the world to shame the wise; God chose the weak things of the world to shame the strong. He chose the lowly things and the despised things—and the things that are not—to nullify the things that are, so that no one may boast before him. (1:27-29)

Gideon's Circumstances

Gideon was called to save his country in an hour of desperate need. Because of idolatry God had permitted the Israelites to fall into the hands of the oppressors, and the Midianites swarmed the whole land from south to north, consuming the produce of the people's toil, blighting the entire country like a plague of locusts and ruling with a rigor so terrible that the Hebrews were driven to seek refuge in the caves and dens of the mountains. All this did not turn them from their sin, for we find that the family of Gideon was idolaters, and there were a grove and shrine of Baal in the little town where he lived. His own personal and social position was insignificant, his family was poor in Manasseh and he was the least in his father's house. He seems to have enjoyed a little exemption from the incursions of the enemy, for when the story opens he had a farm and 10 servants and had succeeded in raising a little grain; but this he had to hide with great caution from the lynx eyes of his prowling oppressors.

The figure he cuts as the panorama begins is not a very brave one. He was hiding behind his winepress as he threshed his grain to conceal it from the Midianites. There is not much in this picture that looks like the germ of a heroic life and yet it was this man, under these depressing circumstances, whom Jehovah called to lead one of the grandest exploits of war. It is still true that our difficulties cannot hinder us and our feebleness cannot defeat us if we are but willing that God should use and control us.

His Call

Suddenly the angel of the Lord appeared to him with a startling message that seemed to mock him: "The LORD is with you, mighty warrior" (Judges 6:12). The words must have made Gideon think of his attitude at the moment.

Skulking behind his barn from his watchful foe he certainly did not seem to be a mighty warrior, and the situation did not look much like the Lord's presence was with them. So he answered quite naturally, "If the LORD is with us, why has all this happened to us? . . . the LORD has abandoned us and put us into the hand of Midian" (6:13). Gideon was looking at his circumstances and himself. When we do this, God's Word never seems true. But the peculiar glory of the grace of Christ is that it declares the sinner to be what he is not, and then it makes him so. It takes the helpless and worthless vessel and fills it with divine life and strength, and then calls it by the new name which the power of God has made true, even though naturally and humanly it would be false. The Word of God creates what it commands. When Christ says to any of us, "You are already clean because of the word I have spoken to you" (John 15:3), you are clean. When He says, "no condemnation" (Romans 8:1) there is none, though there has been a lifetime of sin before. And when He says we have "divine power to demolish strongholds" (2 Corinthians 10:4), then the weak are strong. Faith takes God at His word and then expects Him to make it real.

Let us take God's creating word of justification, power and deliverance, and thus make real the mighty promise, "He gives strength to the weary and increases the power of the weak. . . . but those who hope in the LORD will renew their strength" (Isaiah 40:29, 31).

God therefore was patient with Gideon's unbelief, as He has been with ours, and He helped
him to understand the great secret of accepting
the divine strength. And so we are told He looked
upon Gideon and said, "Go in the strength you
have and save Israel" (Judges 6:14). That look was
an inspiration and it flashed into his soul the very
life of God, as it bid him to go, not in his own
strength but in the new might which God had
just imparted. Of him who walks in the light of
His countenance it is said. "For you are their
glory and strength, and by your favor you exalt
our horn" (Psalm 89:17).

But even yet Gideon hesitated and gave one
more look at himself and his people: "My clan is
the weakest in Manasseh, and I am the least in my
family" (Judges 6:15). He was still thinking of his
human resources. But God once more answered
with the same mighty word He had given to
Moses, "I will be with you" (6:16). He was saying,
"It matters nothing about your family or about
you. I am all you need and certainly I will be with
you and so ample will be your resources that 'you
will strike down all the Midianites together'
(6:16)."

All that God wants of any of us is room for
Himself, the displacement of our self-consciousness and strength in sufficient measure to let Him
have His way without resistance and interference.
The very fact of our absolute helplessness, when
thoroughly learned, makes us willing to give Him
His full way, because there is really nothing we

can do except to let Him work in us to will and do of His good pleasure. Therefore God has to break us down completely before He can use us effectively. The old Moses and gray-haired Caleb and dishonored Peter and halting Jacob and obscure Gideon become the things by which He brings to nothing the pride and strength of earth and hell.

Gideon's Preparation

There was one thing which had to be settled before Gideon went forth with confidence, and that was his own personal acceptance with God. And so he brought to the angel of the Lord an offering and a sacrifice, and as he presented it upon the rock, the flame—symbolic of God's presence—leaped from the rock and devoured the offering and the Lord departed in the fire. Gideon was immediately consumed with dread, the old fear of the unreconciled heart, and he expected immediately to die because he had seen the angel of the Lord. But God reassured the trembling heart and gave him His peace and blessing, and so Gideon commemorated the spot by calling it "Jehovah-shalom"—the Lord will send peace. Perhaps in his simple sacrifice he saw dimly some foreshadowing of the great atonement and knew that his guilt was not imputed, and henceforth he was reconciled and accepted.

This is indispensable to all effective testimony. We must know, and we all may know, that through the blood of Christ we have peace with

God and are justified freely from all things by His grace. Thus our peace has a settled and changeless foundation, and we can say as we go forth to work for others, "I know that I am saved." Have we reared our altar to the God of Peace, and with a heart at rest and in the full assurance of faith, are we able to bring others to the Savior that we have learned so fully to know?

The Beginning of His Work

Gideon's service commenced in his father's house. Our work for God must always begin at home. It is the hardest place, but therefore it must not be left behind us. Gideon's first work was to cut down the grove of Baal in Abiezer and sacrifice one of his father's oxen unto the Lord. He tore down the false and erected the true altar in his own house. He knew it was a perilous attempt, so God indulged him in a little caution, allowing him to go by night with 10 servants of his household. The next morning the men of the village found out the perpetrator of the bold offense and demanded his death. Probably Gideon had felt that his father would be his bitterest foe, especially when he found that he had lost his property, but to his surprise, no doubt, Joash was the first to vindicate him and ironically suggested that if Baal is good for anything as a god, he should be able to take care of himself and settle his accounts with Gideon directly, and as he has not done so he is not disposed to give up his son to their retribution. They seemed to have felt the force of the old man's humor and really made up their minds that Gideon was right (6:25-32).

How often when we take a bold step for God we find our fears all disappointed and our foes all turned into friends! How often the very members of our family, whom we supposed would have been most opposed to us, have been saved by the step that we took in the face of their prejudices! How is it in our homes? Is the altar of Baal destroyed and the altar of God erected? We cannot do much for others until we have been true in the place where God has planted us, and these very difficulties are but the providential opportunity both for our education and for our victory.

Gideon's Larger Work

Proved in his own home, he was then called to save his country. His first step was to make sure of his divine leading. It is true God had already most plainly called him and left no room for doubt in this regard, but his next step was one of tremendous responsibility and he wanted to be absolutely certain that he was in God's way and will. In this he was right. If there was a shadow of doubt it was candid and wise of him to acknowledge and settle it before going further. God is not displeased with us for waiting until He gives us ample assurance of His will, so that when we step out it may be irrevocable.

The method that Gideon took to learn more certainly the will of God, that is, by a sign, is not God's ordinary way for guiding His people now.

It is substantially the same as the lot, and was occasionally resorted to in ancient times, apparently by the divine sanction; but the only time it is mentioned in the New Testament is with implied disapproval. The choosing of Matthias to fill the place of Judas, although done by the apostolic company with a solemn appeal to God, does not appear to have been ever afterwards recognized by God, or Matthias acknowledged as one of the apostles by any divine seal. The Holy Spirit and the Holy Scriptures are so fully given us to point out the will of God that we do not need to resort to this method of direction. God is pleased when His people really trust Him and are willing to obey Him. But in order to make His way plain to them He still sometimes gives various tokens when asked without presumption and in the spirit of faith and full obedience. The one thing in which Gideon's act is unmistakably clear as a pattern for us is in the fact of his becoming certain before stepping forward. The secret of faith and victory is to be sure of our way and then go forward unfalteringly. For two nights he waited before the Lord and the answer was unmistakable on both occasions. Then he stepped forward without a lingering question to face any difficulty or enemy that might confront him.

Purposes that have thus been formed upon our knees and in humble, patient waiting upon the Lord will stand the test of difficulty and delay and are better and surer than all the flashes of impulsive zeal. The secret of many failures lies in the fact that they are experiments rather than acts of faith. "By faith the [Hebrews] passed through the Red Sea as on dry land," without a battle or a doubt, "but when the Egyptians tried to do so, they were drowned" (Hebrews 11:29). There is an infinite difference between *trying* and *believing*.

The next step in Gideon's campaign was the preparation of his army. Thirty-two thousand men had rallied to his standard in answer to his trumpet call. The heroic soul will always find numbers of hearts ready to respond, waiting for some bold spirit to take the initiative. But they are all as yet untried, and untried men are never used in the battles of faith. The only spirits that can stand in the place of battle and on the ground of faith are those that God has fully tested. But God sifted the 32,000. The first objection to them was that they were too many. So vast a company would be in danger of claiming the victory through their own strength, and so God sifted them through their fears and told Gideon to command all the timid and hesitating ones to return to their homes. Twenty-two thousand were only too glad to accept the offer and go back. This is no unusual proportion in the experience of Christian work in every age. But the next objection was that they were too mixed. The instruments through whom God works must not only be brave but also qualified, and so God tested them next by a very simple token which none of them for a moment suspected. It is thus He is always testing us. The simplest acts of our lives show our real character and often determine God's choice or rejection of us for higher service.

As they crossed the stream Gideon was commanded to watch the way in which they stooped to drink. They who did so recklessly, going down on their knees and putting their lips to the stream, were at once set aside as too rash and unwatchful for such an enterprise. Only those who drank from their palms, with eye and mind alert to watch the approaching foe or be ready for any emergency, were chosen. The spirit of intense and whole-hearted devotion to our work so that even the cravings of our physical wants are not permitted to turn us aside or unfit us for our duty has always been the prime requisite for useful service. The good soldier is one whose single idea is to be ever ready for service and to whom privation, hunger, thirst and loss of sleep and comfort are nothing as compared with the chances of battle and the opportunities of victory.

And so in Christ's service men and women who are going to be turned aside from the Master's work by any inconvenience, discomfort or personal interest will never be enrolled among God's 300. How solemn are the tests of life! Let us walk as those who remember that the fretting and murmuring which escape our lips about some trifling inconvenience or the self-interest which turns us aside for an hour from what may be a great opportunity of service are perhaps deciding the issues of our life. Let us be instant in season and out of season, so God can fully trust us and gloriously use us to fight the battles and win the triumphs out of which we are weaving every day our everlasting crowns.

The leader prepared, the army selected, the conflict speedily followed. It was one of the battles of faith, 300 against hundreds of thousands. The resources, humanly speaking, were utterly inadequate; the weapon was the sword of the Lord and of Gideon and the great lesson the strength of weakness when possessed and controlled by Omnipotence. The weapons employed were as insignificant in themselves as the soldiers who used them. Lamps, pitchers and trumpets were all the artillery of this strange campaign. The pitchers were probably earthen vessels, swinging loosely in the hands of the soldiers, and containing inside the lamp or torch which blazed out in the darkness the moment the pitcher was broken, and the trumpet no doubt was a rude instrument of ram's horn, with no music in its tones and serving simply to sound the blast of alarm and the summons of attack. But the use of these simple instruments was exceedingly wise and divinely directed. The little army was posted around a circle enclosing the camp of the enemy, the men stationed equal distances apart.

First, however, Gideon was sent by the Lord to reconnoiter and permitted to overhear, as he lay concealed in the darkness, the terrified words of his enemies, as God had already thrown over them the shadow of their coming fate. In a troubled dream one of the Midianites had already seen a prophecy of their impending defeat, and Gideon heard his own name mentioned as a dread of the foe. Returning hastily to his camp with his heart encouraged by the divine token, he prepared for action. The little army was arranged in the appointed cordon, the watchword whispered to every ear, the lamp lighted in each earthen pitcher, the trumpet ready and the heart of every man, no doubt, lifted to heaven in prayer for God to work through man's feeble instruments.

Then the signal was given. A long sharp trumpet blast resounding round the camp from every trumpet and prolonged in weird and startling notes terrified the sleepers who sprang to their feet and struggled in vain to find in what direction the foe was coming, for on every side was heard that awful cry. Then followed a crash, like the sound of massed artillery, as the pitchers were dashed together in concert and broken into fragments with an unearthly sound, while instantly there blazed upon their vision from every point of the compass a circle of light and fire. High above every sound rang out the concerted shout, "A sword for the LORD and for Gideon!" (Judges 7:20).

The Midianites were thrown into utter panic and confusion, and terror took possession of every heart. Expecting the foe in every direction, they did not recognize their friends in the confusion, and they fell upon one another and beat each other down in desperation and madness, until the whole camp was turned into a scene of

carnage and self-destruction. Those who succeeded in breaking away were pursued by the victorious and orderly hosts of Gideon, and the
pursuit was followed up, until the last fragments
and 120,000 had fallen before the "sword of the
LORD and of Gideon" (KJV).

It was indeed the battle of the Lord. And yet
because heaven fought so mightily on Gideon's
side he did not the less follow up the advantage,
but pressed the conflict to the very last, until the
victory was complete. It was "the word of the
Lord" in the most literal sense, the triumph of
divine power alone; and yet the instruments
employed were both adapted and turned to the
very highest account by human faithfulness and
skill, teaching us that when we trust the Lord
most absolutely, we should follow up His work
most faithfully and use most wisely the feeble
resources which He is pleased to employ.

The Symbolism

Christian faith has delighted to trace in
Gideon's weapons the symbols of those agencies
which the Holy Spirit still employs in the conflict
of Christ's kingdom. The lamp may well suggest
the light of truth when kindled especially in the
heart by the fire of the Holy Spirit. The earthen
pitcher is God's own picture of the frail human
vessel in which God is pleased to enshrine His
light and presence, and it is only when the vessel
is broken that the Lord shines out and reveals not
the instrument, but the Lord Himself. The trum-

pet is the word of our testimony, God's appointed weapon for victory, both in our personal
conflicts and our service for His kingdom. A
broken and empty vessel, revealing in the death
of self the light and love of Christ, and proclaiming His name and word, has been God's weapon
of warfare in all the ages, "divine power to
demolish strongholds" (2 Corinthians 10:4).

It is a great thing thus to learn to depend upon
God to work through our feeble resources, and
yet, while so depending, to be absolutely faithful
and diligent, and not allow our trust to
deteriorate into supineness and indolence. We
find no sloth or negligence in Gideon or his 300;
though they were weak and few, they were wholly
true, and everything in them ready for God to use
to the very last. "Faint, yet pursuing" was their
watchword as they followed and finished their
glorious victory, and they didn't rest until the last
of their enemies was destroyed, and even their
false friends were punished for their treachery
and unfaithfulness.

So God still calls the weakest instruments, but
when He chooses and enables them, they are no
longer weak, but "mighty through God" (10:4,
KJV), and faithful through His grace to every
trust and opportunity; "trusting," as Dr. Chal-
mers would say, "as though all depended upon
God, and working as though all depended on
themselves."

Unfortunately Gideon's latter life did not wholly maintain the high level of this glorious tri-

umph. At the close of the campaign against the Midianities, the grateful people offered to make him their king, but Gideon had grace and loyalty enough to refuse the proffered honor and wisely answered, "The LORD will rule over you" (Judges 8:23). Gideon, however, acted as their judge during his lifetime and wisely administered, in most respects, the government of his people. But in one respect he left a humiliating blemish upon his record and showed how deeply fixed the spirit of idolatry still was among the people and how slowly they learned the lessons of their terrible chastening. He soon established in his own home an image of idolatry and set the example which became a snare to all his people and left the door open for the undoing of all his own life work in the relapse of Israel into the same sins which had brought them the sore oppression from which he had saved them. When he was gone, he left a heritage of strife and misery from which later leaders had once more to deliver the people. His life had risen to the height of one glorious achievement, but alas, he did not know the secret of abiding. The blessed Holy Spirit had not come in that indwelling fullness and keeping grace and power which we enjoy. His glorious career is a sample of what the grace of God can do for the weakest and most helpless who will trust Him fully, and the clearer teachings of the New Testament show us how that grace may become sufficient to sustain us in abiding communion, power and victory.

These achievements were not the result of human effort but were all attributed to the faith of Gideon, and faith is simply that which takes hold of the promise and the fullness of Christ. For us, still greater resources are provided, and for us, the annals of eternity are now being prepared when our lives will shine for the ages to come—as Gideon's for us—as memorials of what the grace of God can do. How much will we take of the fullness and use for His kingdom and glory? As we read these lines, let us be impelled by the heavenly vision to stand up in his place, and clothed with the might of heaven, trained in the discipline of faith and following in the footsteps of our great Captain, take the watchword to ourselves. "The LORD is with you, mighty warrior. . . . Go in the strength you have" (6:12, 14).

CHAPTER 12

David

Lessons from a Good Man's Faults

After removing Saul, he made David their king. He testified concerning him: "I have found David son of Jesse a man after my own heart; he will do everything I want him to do." (Acts 13:22)

Many have wondered why a character so stained with glaring crimes as David's should hold so high a place in sacred biography—among the scriptural patterns of saintliness and service, and even the types of our Lord Jesus Christ Himself. The reason is, that notwithstanding all his inexcusable faults and glaring sins, the deep and uniform purpose of his heart and current of his life were toward God. His errors were not willful acts of disobedience but sudden and passionate outbursts of his own impulsive nature, thoroughly repented of as soon as recognized, and even sanctified to his own soul in developing a deeper holiness and a more watchful obedience.

Therefore God could say of David that he was "a man after my own heart; he will do everything I want him to do" (Acts 13:22). While Saul's one purpose was to please himself, David's highest and uniform aim was to please God. And although he "strayed like a lost sheep" (Psalm 119:176), yet as soon as he heard the Shepherd's voice he gladly followed Him and henceforth walked more closely by His side.

David was foremost a man of faith, and his life is one of the most instructive as well as the most complete examples of the discipline of faith found in the Bible. More full indeed is the picture which the Holy Spirit has given us for this life than of any other in the Old Testament. Like the great Apostle Paul in the New Testament, David's life and character have been unfolded in the double light of his external history and of his internal experience. While the records of Samuel and Chronicles have given us the facts of his history, his incomparable psalms have left us the inner picture of his spiritual struggles and experiences, even as the Pauline Epistles have unfolded the spiritual life of the great apostle coordinately with the story of his life and labors in the Acts of the Apostles.

The Dawn of David's Faith

He was the youngest child of a large family and overshadowed by the more bold and aggressive spirits and more showy qualities of his brothers. Not very much was expected of the youthful stripling; and so while his brothers were trained for military service, he was allowed to choose the simple and uneventful occupation of a shepherd in the fields of Bethlehem. His choice of such a life links him very tenderly with the line of illustrious Hebrew shepherds which began with Abel and included Abraham, Isaac, Jacob and Moses, and was yet to be crowned by the higher office of "that great Shepherd of the sheep" (Hebrews 13:20), who was afterwards to come of David's own line.

The motive for such a preference may have been his simple-hearted love of nature and God and his enjoyment of the stillness and communion which his work afforded. No doubt it was in these days of seclusion and meditation that the spirit of poetic genius was first awakened and the keynotes of his sublime psalms were whispered to his listening heart.

We have some hints in these psalms of the origin of his early piety. Although we don't know her name, yet there is scarcely a doubt that David owed his earliest religious impressions to his mother's faith and piety. In some of his prayers he appeals to her God in language which leaves no doubt as to her religious character and of its influence upon his earliest recollections. It is said that John Newton, in his most reckless moments, when suddenly brought face to face with danger and impending death, used to pray, "Oh, God, my mother's God, have mercy on me." In the same spirit David cries,

"O LORD . . . I am your servant, the son of your maidservant; you have freed me from my chains" (Psalm 116:16), and again, "save the son of your maidservant" (86:16). Such testimony is higher honor than a splendid name and a long record. She lived in her illustrious son as a true mother loves to do.

David's faith in God had early opportunities of proving itself in the circumstances of his simple life. When afterwards explaining to Saul his confidence in the result of his duel with Goliath, he stated how once, in his shepherd days, a lion and a bear came out of the thicket and seized a lamb from his flock, and how, in the name of his God, he had attacked the intruder and rescued the prey from the jaws of the devourer. And then he gave the glory altogether to God and declared that the same God who delivered him from the lion and the bear would deliver him from the Philistine.

This is very beautiful and instructive. It is doubtful if David would ever have fought Goliath or sat on Judah's throne if he had faltered in this first trial of faith and courage. How very solemn the thought that God is ever testing us for future service in the opportunities and occurrences of our ordinary lives. The smallest difficulty which we allow to overcome us may determine our rejection for higher service because "Whoever can be trusted with very little can also be trusted with much" (Luke 16:10).

The Great Promise of Faith

At length God honored His servant's faith with the mightiest promise of his life. The call to a kingdom and the anointing by Samuel, although a surprise to all his house, found David ready to believe the great message. Accepting with humble faith the mighty promise, he received the special baptism of the Holy Spirit for his future work and from that day recognized himself as God's chosen king.

The opportunity soon came to prove his faith and to exhibit on a larger scale the courage which he had manifested in the defense of his sheepfold at Bethlehem. His battle with Goliath was a miniature of the life-long battle of his faith. It displayed the firm heroic courage and simple trust in which he had been already so well trained in his humble life, and it brought him before his people and sovereign in a light which henceforth changed the whole attitude of his life. In the psalms of this period and of the years that immediately followed, we find David taking the place of a king, and sometimes calling himself by the very title. He fully accepted the promise of God and committed his faith to its fulfillment from that hour. In all these Bible examples of faith, we must have noticed how very distinctly and unmistakably the ground of faith is given in the promise of God.

It is most essential in our conflicts of faith that we have a sure word of prophecy on which to rest, otherwise the struggle will be a very perplexing one. To Moses and Joshua, to David and Gideon, God was pleased to give an unqualified word of promise, so that there was no place for doubt to enter. The secret of our victory must ever be to have under our feet the solid rock of God's immutable Word; then we can stand "though the earth give way and the mountains fall into the heart of the sea, though its waters roar and foam and the mountains quake with their surging" (Psalm 46:2-3).

The Trial of His Faith

As with all the others, David had to be tested, and the test is usually in proportion to the importance of the promise. For nine years David was called to pass through a series of troubles, persecutions and perils, sufficient to destroy a faith less than divine and obliterate the last shred of mere human enthusiasm and sentiment. Every circumstance of his life conspired to contradict the word of promise which God had given and to turn to ridicule the very idea of his kingly claims, until at last he almost gave up in despair and cried in sore perplexity, "One of these days I will be destroyed by the hand of Saul. The best thing I can do is to escape to the land of the Philistines" (1 Samuel 27:1).

This was the one thoroughly weak hour of David's life, and in a moment of unbelief he yielded to fear and began to compromise. As always happens, his unbelief led him into many false positions, and for a long time he acted a dissembling part, seeking safety under the guise of pretended madness, and tolerated by the Philistines because he was regarded as irresponsible. At length his policy was brought to a disastrous ending, and returning one day from one of his expeditions, he found his city Ziklag in ashes and the wives and children of him and his men carried captives. It was a dark and trying hour. The men gave way to discouragement and despair and talked of even stoning David. After all, he was the man who had led them into their misfortunes and troubles. They had followed David under the impression that he was a special subject of divine protection, but he had proved to be no better than themselves. God had to let this come to beat David out of his unbelieving experience. When all his resources had been utterly baffled and he had reached the darkest hour, then God met him. When our faith fails us, then God remains and underneath our sinking feet we find the everlasting arms.

And so we find David's faith suddenly recovering its balance. In that dark hour, when all was gloom and despair on the part of others, we read that "David found strength in the LORD his God" (30:6). Committing his case wholly to heaven and asking counsel of the Lord, he pursued and overtook his foes and recovered all the spoil, and best of all, his beloved companions and friends. This was the turning point of his life, and a few days later the dark night of years had passed away, and he found himself in the happy enjoyment of the long deferred promises of God, sitting upon the throne of Judah, without his having to strike a single blow or do anything to injure his cruel, unfortunate rival.

The story of his faith in those trying years is very fully unfolded in his own psalms. In the 27th and 37th Psalms, we have the very keynote of his faith. He has left for us the cheering testimony,

> I am still confident of this:
>> I will see the goodness of the LORD
>> in the land of the living.   (27:13)

> Commit your way to the LORD;
>> trust in him and he will do this:
> He will make your righteousness shine like
>>   the dawn,
>> the justice of your cause like the noonday
>>   sun.   (37:5-6)

Thus indeed He vindicated David's faith, and for nearly half a century he was permitted to look back, and, from his own experience, proclaim to the coming ages the faithfulness of God. The whole 37th Psalm reads like a double picture of his life and the life of Saul. We see the man that brought wicked devices to pass, as at length he faded away and was no more, while David waited upon the Lord and delighted himself in his God and so inherited the earth and delighted in the abundance of peace, sometimes stumbling it is true, but arising again with a glad and thankful shout, "though he stumble, he will not fall, for the LORD upholds him with his hand" (37:24).

And so the web of David's life was woven with the mingled threads of sorrow and joy. All of us must learn the old lesson that God can give us nothing until we have been proved. The first stage, therefore, of every promise is a disappointment and a death. The next is a trust that sings in the night and counts the "things that are not as though they were" (Romans 4:17). The last is the happy and glorious consummation and the song of thanksgiving. "Let us not become weary in doing good, for at the proper time we will reap a harvest if we do not give up" (Galatians 6:9).

> So do not throw away your confidence; it will be richly rewarded. You need to persevere so that when you have done the will of God, you will receive what he has promised. For in just a very little while, "He who is coming will come and will not delay." (Hebrews 10:35-37)

The Victory of Faith

Not only did David's faith find the complete fulfillment of all the promises of God, but it pressed forward into bolder and more aggressive steps. He did not rest down in his blessing as a selfish gratification but used it as a vantage ground for yet higher advances. And so he completed the conquests of his kingdom until he had encompassed it with the ancient boundaries of God's largest promises to Abraham, and had become the head of a dominion outranking the mightiest kingdoms of his time and comparing favorably with the power of Egypt in former centuries or the later empires that followed in Central Asia. He bequeathed to Solomon his son a dominion without a rival, reaching from the Mediterranean to the Euphrates. Not only so, but he strengthened his kingdom by wise administration and a system of government which extended through every department of the public service, and laid a foundation for permanence and prosperity which nothing but the flagrant wickedness of his successors could destroy. Yet higher than all, his chief concern was to consecrate the advantages of his triumph and the resources of his reign to the glory of God and the advancement of His kingdom. Regarding himself simply as a representative of Jehovah, he trained his people to recognize Him as their true Sovereign and made the tabernacle the center of the kingdom. One of his earliest acts was the removal of the ark to Mount Zion and the establishment of the public service on the most elaborate and magnificent scale. The closing years of his kingdom were chiefly given to planning and preparing for the erection of the most splendid monument for public worship ever reared on earth, to which he and his princes personally contributed more than $200 million, and for which he provided from the resources of his kingdom a sum probably equal to $5 billion.

In all these triumphs and achievements we find him constantly recognizing God as the source of his strength, the inspiration of his wisdom and the dependence of all his trust. Even his very battles were not the exploits of a great soldier, but conflicts of faith, as literally as his victory over Goliath with a simple sling and a stone from the valley brook. It was supernatural power that nerved his arm and divine wisdom that planned his strategy, enabling him to say, "It is God who arms me with strength . . . He trains my hands for battle; . . . you stoop down to make me great" (Psalm 18:32, 34, 35).

And still the resources of Christ are equal to all the needs of the most active life, whether it is the pursuit of secular business, the consultations of the statesmen and the public servant, the toil of the artisan or the special service of the Christian worker. All may be the work of faith, the daily memorial of the sufficiency of Christ, and the supernatural grace which He provides for every situation in which His providence has placed us.

The Eclipse of David's Faith

Two acts of glaring and presumptuous sin overshadowed the closing years of David's reign with the deepest gloom and some of the most appalling disasters. One was his double crime of passion and policy in the matter of Uriah and Bathsheba; and the other, his presumptuous numbering of the people under the sudden temptation of pride and conscious power. The first of these was followed by a long train of domestic calamities, culminating in the rebellion and death of Absalom; the second, by the special visitation of divine judgment, which for a moment threatened the extinction of the people. They both, however, brought out the law of faith in marvelous vividness through the heightening contrast of sin and sorrow.

There is nothing more amazing in the records of Christian experience than the truth and delicacy of religious feeling expressed in the 51st Psalm. While on the one hand he takes the place of abject penitence and self-abnegation, realizing sin in its darkest relations; yet on the other, he accepts the mercy of God with unquestioning confidence and recognizes the power of grace not only to forgive, but to obliterate completely every trace of his guilt and corruption and to restore him to spotless purity. With one breath he could cry, "My sin is always before me. . . . Surely I was sinful at birth, . . . Save me from bloodguilt" (51:3, 5, 14); and with another breath, "I will be whiter than snow. . . . Then I will teach transgressors your ways, and sinners will turn back to you" (51:7, 13). It is a difficult thing, and for some natures impossible, to recognize at the same time the full enormity of our guilt and also to accept without doubt the full and free forgiveness of God. The very triumph of the faith of the gospel is that it puts us in the sinner's place without palliation or excuse, and yet lifts us to the place of the justified, of whom even the Holiest can say, "All beautiful you are, . . . there is no flaw in you" (Song of Songs 4:7).

This experience of David's was practically an anticipation of that sanctification which Christ has revealed and the Holy Spirit has brought to us in the gospel. David becomes another example of that deep and radical change which must come to every child of God at some period after justification, and which is always preceded in some form by a deeper conviction of sin than previously experienced. It is beautiful to find that David, one of the most illustrious saints of God in the Old Testament, had the same experience in this regard through which we now pass in the richer grace of God in Christ. The experience of the 51st Psalm is a great deal more than the restoration of a backslider; it is the profound conviction of sin in its natural and original depravity and the acceptance of the grace of Christ in its sanctifying fullness. It was at least a compensation for the shame and sorrow of his fearful fall that it brought David into this deeper experience of the grace of God and lifted him into a place where henceforth he might be sustained and kept by the power of God.

The other cloud which fell on David's life was that of sorrow, and in this also we find his faith equal to the emergency. When the terrible calamity of Absalom's rebellion swept over him, he committed himself calmly to the divine protection. When his enemy cursed him, his meek and patient answer was, "let him curse. . . . It may be that the LORD will . . . repay me with good for the cursing I am receiving this day" (2 Samuel 16:11-12).

When his cruel and unnatural son was seeking his father's life and kingdom, David was far more concerned for Absalom than for himself. And when at last the crowning judgment of heaven was to fall upon the people because of David's act of numbering them and he was given his choice of the form the judgment should take, with beautiful faith he threw himself into the hands of God rather than of man, and meekly yielded himself and his kingdom to the justice and mercy of Jehovah. "Let us fall into the hands of the LORD, for his mercy is great; but do not let me fall into the hands of men" (24:14). Like a child who, when about to be chastised by his father, rushes inside the rod and throws himself into his arms, so that the blow cannot reach him, so David's faith took refuge in the bosom of his God, and the stroke fell more lightly; and when it ceased, the very place of judgment became the memorial of blessing and the site of Solomon's temple. Thus his faith surmounted the difficulties, both of sin and sorrow. For us there is the same sanctification and the same deliverance for all who trust in Him.

The Ministry of David's Faith

The oft erring and sinning servant of the Lord was enabled, notwithstanding the mistakes of his life, to become a blessing, not only to his own generation, but to all succeeding ages of time. His very character and life are a source of encouragement to the children of infirmity and frailty. The fact that God could make so much out of such a broken life may well keep us from discouragement and despair. The reason why God could do all this for David was that his heart was perfect toward God and his purpose true. Blinded once by passion and once by pride, he mistook the way and even lost his own true instincts of righteousness, but the moment his eyes were open he turned, like a penitent child, to the will of God and the more humbly sought to undo his fault and glorify his Lord.

The highest ministry and most glorious testimony of his life was that which even is our noblest service—to hold up Jesus Christ. His own life was honored as a type of the Messiah in a preeminent degree. His birth at Bethlehem, his shepherd calling, his sufferings, his victories, his prophetic and especially his kingly office, were all striking types of his greater Son. In these respects the life of David exhibited to the ages to come the picture of the great Redeemer. Even more than this, his writings were his prophetic visions of the Messiah's sufferings and glory. Nowhere else, as in the 22nd Psalm, have we the innermost view of the dying anguish of the Lamb of God; nowhere else, as in the 72nd Psalm, have we the vision of his millennial glory; and nowhere else have we a more perfect picture of His resurrection, ascension and kingly reign as in the second, 16th, 24th, 68th and 100th Psalms. David was a witness for Christ both in his life and in his testimony. Are we thus witnesses for Him? Are our lives exhibiting Him, and are our lips proclaiming Him to others?

Finally, David has ministered as no other Old Testament character to the consolation of the saints of God. "The Sweet Psalmist of Israel" has led the choirs of all the ransomed as they have passed into Zion with songs of everlasting joy (Isaiah 35:10). He has been the author of their worship and their praise, and his words have become the watchwords of comfort and victory in the night of sorrow and the valley of the shadow of death to countless billions who are singing with him now in the choruses of heaven the song of the Lamb. This ministry, in a humbler measure, may be the recompense of every true and trusting heart.

David's faith turned even his sin and sorrow to the good of others. After his restoration from sin and shame, his one purpose was to teach transgressors God's way and lead sinners to Him. He turned the chords of pain in the harp of life into minor notes in the pilgrim's song, and out of every situation of his life there has come some ministry of blessing to others. The marvelous alchemy of faith is that it turns everything into gold and under its touch sorrow is transfigured, sin is transformed, and even the curse transmuted into a blessing.

CHAPTER 13

Elijah

God's Patience with Failures of His People

Elijah was a man just like us. He prayed earnestly that it would not rain, and it did not rain on the land for three and a half years. Again he prayed, and the heavens gave rain, and the earth produced its crops. (James 5:17-18)

"Elijah was a man just like us" is the last commentary of the New Testament on the greatest of the Old Testament prophets. Instead of dwelling on the strength of his character, the Holy Spirit calls our attention to the infirmities of his faith. It would seem as if God wants us to remember, not so much the greatness of human character, as its helplessness, and dwell rather on the greatness of His grace, magnified by man's very frailties and failures. A life so illustrious as the Prophet of Fire's is apt to become a snare to others, leading us to look at the man rather than his Master, and overshadowing our commonplace lives by the grandeur of his attainments. Therefore, God has often allowed the most illustrious of His saints to fail in their strongest qualities, that they may "stop trusting in man, who has but a breath in his nostrils" (Isaiah 2:22), and learn the sufficiency of God from His transcendent grace, as shown most conspicuously in the weaknesses of His people. Perhaps more hearts have been helped by David's recovery, Peter's restoration and God's patience with Elijah in his ignominious failure, than by all the glorious triumphs of these eminent servants of God.

Let us review the story of Elijah, therefore, not so much with reference to the sublime attainments of his faith, as to the lessons which God would teach us through his weakness and the grace which restored him.

Faith That Boldly Stands Amid Evil

Elijah appeared upon the scene of Hebrew history like a meteor flash. We have no record of his birth or childhood and no trace of the development of the life of faith and the sacred fire of prophetic inspiration. A child of the wilderness, like John the Baptist, his character was molded in solitary communion with nature and God and developed those stern and rugged qualities which peculiarly fitted him for the ministry of judgment to which he was specially called. Like a lightning stroke he fell across the path of the wicked Ahab and, with a formula of prophetic introduction peculiar to himself, proclaimed in the name of Jehovah, the long-forgotten God of the Israelites, the beginning of a period of judgment which was soon to leave the land a blighted scene of desolation. Just as suddenly he disappeared, and for the years that followed no trace was found of him, although he was eagerly sought by the troubled king in every corner of the land. Such an apparition so terrible, followed by the threatened judgment, was enough to stamp his figure on the minds of all succeeding ages. Such a message and such a ministry required and exhibited the highest faith. It implied a confidence in God and courageous disdain of man worthy of the loftiest examples of heroic faith. It stands for sublimity, with Joshua's command to the sun to stand still on Gideon, and Hezekiah's prayer that the sun dial should be arrested 10 degrees in the advance of the heavens. The Apostle James implies that this bold act was the result of much earnest prayer and that he did not dare thus to stand before the king and the world and in the name of God hold back the rain, without having first received the answering word from heaven on which true faith must always rest and act.

In this he is an example to us of the faith which stands in courageous boldness against surrounding evil, and claims, from heaven, perhaps not the judgments of a former dispensation, but the overruling power and providence of God for the glory of His name and the interests of His kingdom.

Faith That Is Dependent on God

But we next see Elijah's faith in a new aspect, that is, in dependence on God for his own needs and the needs of those dependent upon him in those days of fiery trial.

First, we find him at the little brook in the wilderness, fed by ravens and dependent on God for his daily bread, with a trust which has often encouraged the struggling and needy saints of God. Next, we see his faith exposed to a keener pressure, when he was required by the Lord to take the last handful of meal and drop of oil from the starving widow and her child. It is easier to suffer want ourselves than to see others suffer on our account. This God required from Elijah, and he in turn required of the widow of Zarephath that she also should so learn the lesson of trust that she could give her last crumb to the servant of God. Thus it was that the daily miracle began, and the little household at Zarephath became an example of what has so often since been proved in the homes of the poor, that "Better a little with the fear of the LORD than great wealth with turmoil" (Proverbs 15:16).

At length one step of faith leads to a higher. We never trust God for a little thing but He honors us by letting us receive a greater. And so the faith of Elijah and the widow for their daily bread was at length honored in what was the most stupendous miracle up to that point in human history—the raising of her lifeless boy from the dead. Little do we dream when we begin to trust God for little things that these are stepping-stones on which we are treading to higher glories and victories, not only in this life but in the ages to come, when the lessons of faith we are learning today will be exemplified on a grander theater and a sublimer scale. This glorious miracle, which was also given in answer to prayer, might well prepare the mighty prophet for the great test which would immediately follow.

Faith and the Prophets of Baal

And so his faith was next tried on the grandest occasion and the most majestic exhibition of Old Testament history. Suddenly appearing before the king, he summoned him and his people to meet him on Mount Carmel for a decisive trial of the great question between God and Baal. The summons was met by an extraordinary convocation, the people coming together in tens of thousands. The 800 prophets and priests of Baal and the king himself were all there on the one side, and Elijah alone on the other. The test which he proclaimed was simply and absolutely fair. Every advantage was given to the other side; the representatives of Baal were allowed to begin and the entire day was given to them for the purpose of proving their claims and obtaining some answering token from their idols. At length when the evening shades began to gather and they had ignominiously failed in every attempt and tried in vain by cries and mutilations to bring some answer from their gods, Elijah dismissed them with contempt and stepped forward to claim the answer of Jehovah. His appeal was a very simple one. The old altar of former years was prepared; the bleeding sacrifice was laid upon it. To make the test doubly difficult, a deep trench was dug on every side and water was poured over the altar and trenches until they were flooded in every direction. Then he lifted his eyes to heaven and addressed his simple prayer. It was but a few sentences; he calmly asked Jehovah to vindicate Himself and His prophet and make the people understand that He is God. There was no strain or pleading; this had already been done. His faith was so confident that he needed but speak his request.

His words had scarcely ceased, when suddenly the gathering twilight was lit up with the quivering flash of heavenly fire; the altar was ablaze with the devouring flame; the hissing tongues of lambent fire licked up the water in the trenches, while a strange awe and stillness held the breath of the amazed spectators. Then there came the tumultuous reaction and a great shout rose up from every side, prolonged and repeated from rank to rank, and echoed back from Carmel's rocks and caves again and again. "The LORD—he is God!" (1 Kings 18:39). But Elijah did not lose his self-command for a moment. The trial was over, the verdict was announced, the people had turned back to their God, but the judgment was now to be revoked. So, speaking again in the language of audacious faith, he proclaimed to the king that the heavens were about to open and the clouds to burst, and bade him to prepare for his journey, "for there is the sound of a heavy rain" (18:41).

There was as yet no sound, except in the prophet's ear, and the only sound that he had heard was the sound of the people's shout and the anticipations of his own faith. But faith always seeks its message before sense confirms it! And so Elijah hastened to his watchtower to press upon Jehovah the claim which he had already announced and to wait for the first signal. There, bowed down before God, with his face between his knees in the attitude of a travailing mother, he agonized in the prayer of the Spirit. So real did it appear to him that he felt that there must be some cloud upon the sky and he sent his servant again and again to report; but there was none. But the ear of faith cannot be deceived, the faith of God cannot be a lie; something must give way when the Holy Spirit thus prays. And so Elijah waited and prayed, not in the agony of doubt, but in the triumphant energy of the power, and at last, the seventh time when the process of faith was accomplished, the message came, "a cloud as small as a man's hand is rising from the sea" (18:44). Was it a fitting emblem of the hand of Elijah which was moving the heavens, or was it the hand of Jesus which his hand had grasped? It was enough at least, and springing to his feet he hastened back to the king and bid him at once depart for his palace.

Girding up his loins, he dashed on before like a victorious captain leading the triumphal march of a nation, while the heavens became black with clouds, and the floods of rain would have even filled the people with alarm had they not been too full of gladness and gratitude to be appalled, even by the wildest fury of the tempest.

Faith Often Fails Following Victory

Up to the gates of Jezreel the enthusiastic prophet sped. There he halted while Ahab hurried in. His victory was complete, his faith was vindicated; what need that he should go further? Ah, was not this the moment of danger? Can we help regretting that he did not pass through those gates and face that defiant queen who alone remained unconquered, but whose imperious will was the real barrier of adamancy against which the whole battle was directed? Was not this the one unfinished battle, the one of fatal omission? Was there perhaps, for the first time, one thought of timidity, one cowardly impulse, one procrastinating dream, that the rest could be finished tomorrow? At least we know that before the next day's sun had risen, the desperate spirit of the queen had met the tide of rebellion with victorious defiance, and even Elijah himself was fleeing back like a wave from the unyielding shore, leaving all the work of his life apparently undone. Truly there is no hour so full of peril as the hour of triumph.

If conqueror, of tomorrow's fight, beware;
If conquered, for tomorrow's fight, prepare.

Elijah's failure was as sudden and complete as his triumph had been bold and startling. There was an entire reaction, and the man of flint and fire was broken as a potter's vessel and feeble as a fretting child. One fierce, defiant word from Jezebel, gleaming like the savage lightning and threatening with a doom as swift and terrible as her murdered prophets before another sun had set, hurled him in a moment from the pinnacle of triumph to the depths of agonizing terror, and "Elijah was afraid and ran for his life" (19:3). One thought alone took possession of the paralyzed prophet, to flee and save himself. And yet, when he got beyond her reach and sank exhausted in the desert, with a strange inconsistency of weakness and fear, he actually asked that he might die. If this was what he wanted he had an excellent chance to do it nobly in Samaria. What sad work the devil can make of poor humanity when God lets us go for an instant! After poor Elijah, no heart need ever feel discouraged.

Why did he fall? Was it because he did not go far enough and finish his work with Jezebel's destruction too? Perhaps so, and if so, it is another solemn lesson of the peril of the half-finished work of faith and obedience which stops within a fraction of the fullness of God's will. Or was it because he depended too much on the effect of God's judgment and was disappointed to find that, after all, the spirit of human pride and wickedness was still unchanged? Or was it, more than all this, because Elijah had allowed his own self-consciousness to assume too high a place, and like Simon Peter, had to fail in order to experience the death of self? Was Elijah a little in his own way, as Jonah afterward was in the way of another of the prophets of the Lord? It must have been so. That bitter cry, "I am no better than my ancestors" (19:4), lets out the secret. He seemed astonished to find his own weakness. He had never been any better than his fathers even in the height of his triumph, and it was only the grace of God in him that accomplished what it did. But somehow, he must have become absorbed in his own greatness and got in God's way so much that he had to be humiliated and slain, and then with the deeper lesson of self-crucifixion, sent back to finish his work. Is not this the secret of almost all our failures and has not God decreed that he that trusts in man will ever fall until he learns to lean, not upon Elijah, but upon Elijah's God?

God's Gentleness in Our Failure

Notice the gentleness of God in picking up and setting on his feet once more His broken child. He saw that part of his desperate collapse was due to physical causes; his body and brain had been under a tremendous strain for days and even years, and looking away for a moment from God the pressure had become too great. And so the first thing that God did was to rest and nurse him

like a sick and weary child. He put him to sleep
under the juniper tree and then gently awakened
him and fed his weary body. Later He bid him to
rise again and waking him once more, made him
eat again of the heavenly meal before he set out
on his journey across the desert.

How kindly God cares for our bodies as well as
our spirits, and how often He says to His fretting
children, "Come away and rest awhile," and gently strengthens and refreshes them before sending
them forth to bear the heavy burdens of life. He
who was moved with compassion for the hungry
multitudes and who Himself suffered hunger and
was sorely tempted by the devil, still knows the
frailty of our frame and ministers to our bodies as
well as to our spirits.

Next we notice how God took His child apart
with Himself to the desert for a while and there
talked with him and taught him the lessons which
he needed to learn. So often He calls us aside
from our work for a season and bids us be still
and learn before we go forth again to minister.
Especially is this so when there has been some
serious break, sudden failure or radical defect in
our work.

There is no time lost in such waiting hours.
Fleeing from his enemies, an ancient knight
found that his horse needed to be reshod.
Prudence seemed to urge him on without delay,
but higher wisdom taught him to halt a few
minutes at the blacksmith's forge by the way to
have the shoe replaced, and although he heard

the feet of his pursuers galloping hard behind, yet he waited those minutes until his charger was refitted for his flight, and then, leaping into his saddle just as they appeared a hundred yards away, he dashed away from them with the fleetness of the wind, and knew that his halting had hastened his escape. So often God bids us wait before we go in order to fully recover ourselves for the next great stage of the journey and work.

But again, God spoke to His servant and set him thinking and examining his heart and life. "What are you doing here, Elijah?" (19:9). God's best way of teaching us is to ask us questions and God is asking many of us, "What are you doing here?" Elijah was not very ready to listen to the question and was too quick to answer in the words of hasty vindication, as we so often are. Let us pause and think whether we are where God wants us fully, especially if there is in our life some great and serious failure. If our faith and courage have given way, and we have gone back in any way from our trust, let us not be too ready to blame our enemies or reflect upon our God and vindicate ourselves, but see if there is not something lacking with us and some lesson God tenderly waits to teach us.

Elijah's Lesson

But next, we notice, very distinctly, the lesson which God insisted on having His prophet learn. This great self-conscious "I" had to be slain and Elijah had to learn that he was by no means the only faithful follower of Jehovah in Israel and not at all indispensable to the great work which he supposed had all been resting on his shoulders. God told him that there were 7,000 in Israel who had not bowed the knee to the image of Baal or in any way compromised their testimony and dishonored their God, and that He had abundant instruments besides him through whom He could work. He concluded by sending him to call three instruments to finish the work which he had begun and left so sadly unfinished.

One of those was Hazael, the future king of Syria, a foreign soldier whom God could use at His pleasure to fulfill His purposes and punish His wicked people. Another was Jehu, an unknown captain in the army of Ahab, who was to succeed him as king in a little while. A third was Elisha, a humble farmer in the fields of Samaria, who was to be Elijah's servant and successor, and in his life and quiet ministry to accomplish much more in the destruction of idolatry and the establishing of God's kingdom than even Elijah himself. All this must have humbled Elijah in the dust and made him feel how easy it was for God to take him at his word and let him die, if need be, and have others arise at God's bidding and accomplish His unfailing purposes.

How infinite are God's resources, and how insignificant any one of His instrumentalities in itself! God cannot use us much until we learn that if He does use us at all, it is not because of our importance, but His great condescension in per-

mitting us to be workers together with Him. No
man is of much account in God's service until he
learns not to place much value on himself. It was
an awful stripping of the greatest of the prophets
but it was indispensable for him to learn. His
work did not cease. He went forth from Horeb to
many years of honored service and passed at
length with unparalleled honor and glory to his
great reward. But his work henceforth was more
quiet and modest, and he himself was out of
sight. Even his translation to heaven, with all its
majestic surroundings, was almost entirely
withdrawn from the gaze of men and would have
been even from Elisha's had not the latter insisted upon witnessing it. Henceforth Elijah's
death was over, and his funeral past, and there
awaited only his translation. It was worth all the
humiliation of the desert to learn this lesson.

But again, God taught him in his restoration
the insufficiency of mere judgment and all the influences of law and terror to change and purify
the human heart. He taught him the need of that
gentler dispensation of divine grace and spiritual
power which was to follow Elijah's own fiery
ministry in the spirit and work of Elisha, and
which was, at a later period, to be introduced in
all its fullness by the Lord Jesus Christ, of whom
Elisha was to be a special type. And so God took
him through a sort of panorama in the cave of
Horeb which was to symbolize this special truth.

All the terrific forces of nature passed before
him, the symbols of his own fiery spirit and God's

most awful judgments. The whirlwind came first.
The heavens grew black as midnight, the fiery
lightnings rent the inky clouds and the thunders
rose in a roar. Like a giant arm, the tempest
struck the forests and swept them as the scythe of
the mower. The very rocks were torn from their
lofty bases and hurled into the abyss. The desert
sand was caught up in great clouds to meet the
denser masses of the sky. The giant hand of the
storm gathered in its fists the mingled column of
cloud, sand, rocks and trees, and hauled it along
as projectiles from the cannon's mouth, sweeping
from its track everything that resisted, leaving a
path of wreckage and desolation, while the
mingled roar and shriek of the warring elements
and the terrified creatures of the earth and air
blended in an indescribable chorus of terror and
sublimity. The prophet himself had to cling to
the rock for security or perhaps throw himself
upon the ground to escape being swept away. But
his spirit was still unmoved and the Lord was not
in the whirlwind.

The earthquake then shook the solid ground
and heaved the mountains from their bases.
Yawning gulfs burst open at his feet and
avalanches of rocks were hurled into the chasm
below, while the mountain and the desert heaved
like the swelling sea and the sickening roar of the
awful convulsion of nature came from the depths
of the earth and the caves of the mountains. Unmoved, and perhaps defiant, he felt that the Lord
was not in the earthquake.

The phenomenon that followed is not particularly described farther than it is called the fire, but we know it must have been something that would worthily cap the climax and appear yet mightier and more terrific than either the earthquake or the whirlwind. Perhaps it was an awful display of electric wonders, a play of lightning and thunder such as sometimes follows the first fury of the wind and lasts often for hours, in which the whole heaven seems to be one mass of flame and the earth sends up to meet it a ceaseless fire of electric artillery, until the whole air seems to melt with fervent heat and the thunderbolts of heaven fall like the fire of innumerable batteries. An eastern sky can produce a thunderstorm that might well be called a rain of fire.

Or the phenomenon may have been a display more supernatural, of the very blaze of the same fiery tongues that had fallen on the sacrifice on Carmel, or on the rebellious company of Datham and Abiram, or the cities of Sodom and Gomorrah, or afterwards in the ministry of Elijah himself upon the soldiers who came to take him captive. At least we may be sure it was a display of surpassing magnificence and awful terror. It was a peculiar manifestation of the angry judgment of Jehovah which will at last destroy the wicked. But even this Elijah felt, perhaps to his own astonishment, had no effect on his spirit. In the heat of the desperate bitterness of his soul the divine judgment could not move him, and he found, it may be for the first time, that the human heart can look upon the very terrors of Jehovah's judgment and yet remain as hard as ever. The most awful fact in human experience is that the judgments of God do not change men's hearts. The terrors of Sinai did not save Israel from their carnival of idolatry before the month was past. The repeated judgments of God upon His ancient people did not hold them back from the grossest idolatry. The unparalleled horrors to which the Hebrew race has been exposed throughout all the centuries have not made them Christians. Nor will the very punishment of the Judgment Day and the eternal torments of an everlasting hell; but the lips of sinners will curse back again in answer to their judgments and the ages of eternity will doubtless increase the wickedness and malignity of the lost.

The time had come for God to reveal to Elijah the true secret of power. The elements were hushed, an awful stillness fell upon the scene, and out of the midst of it came a voice faint as a whisper of the gentlest breeze. A voice which fell perhaps on his own ear—one of those deep, strange instincts of unutterable quietness and yet deepest tenderness, a thrill which reached Elijah's inmost being, wooed his spirit into adoration and brought to his whole consciousness a sense of God and His ineffable presence and glory. It was something which penetrated every fiber of his being, which melted his heart into tenderness and his spirit into submission, until he gathered his mantle around him and went into his cave to hear the voice which alone could satisfy and fill his being.

The power which alone can affect the hearts of men is God Himself. Elijah felt it in his inmost being and then he knew how little were all his denunciations and strokes of punishment without the Spirit of the Holy One to move upon the hearts of men.

And so he was prepared in a measure for the announcements which immediately followed, bidding him to appoint two men as the messengers of judgment, but especially the third who was to be the prophet of grace, whose very name signifies the salvation of God, and who is the type of Jesus Christ and His ministry of love. Elijah was the ax and the flame which cleared the forest; Elisha, the sower and the gentle rain and sunshine that nurtured the seed. Elijah was the winter frost that withered the false growth of centuries; Elisha, the springtime of better age, with its blossoms and fruits of life and righteousness.

But even Elisha was but a type and shadow of a greater than he, who has come to baptize with the Holy Spirit and to enable poor, weak, lost men, in His strength, to fulfill the righteousness which the law could show but could not give. Thank God, we live in that better age and have that heavenly voice enshrined, through the indwelling Comforter, in the sanctuary of our hearts! Let us not forget Elijah's lesson, both in the struggle with our own spirits and the principles of our work for the salvation of men and the elevation of society. This is the vital principle of Christianity, which is a work of grace and not of judgment, of the Divine Spirit and of God Himself, and not the struggle and efforts of human nature.

The All-Sufficiency of God

The last lesson taught Elijah in his recovery and taught also to all future ages is the all-sufficiency of God and the wretched insufficiency of the best of men. Elijah's failure had magnified the grace of Elijah's God, while it had minified Elijah himself. Henceforth men could accomplish the mightiest purposes through the grace which is as free to the feeblest saint as to the mightiest prophet. This is especially the lesson that we need to learn. The God of Elijah is our God, and the grace which he received is offered freely to every one of us in the measure of our need and our trust. There is nothing that God has ever done for any ransomed saint which He is not willing to do for any other who will trust Him and glorify Him. Elijah has passed away, but Elijah's God remains. Elijah's faith, even, for a season vanished, but Elijah's God changed not. Oh, how blessed to know that when our own faith fails us, there is One who changes not, and whose faithfulness survives the frailties of our nature and holds us in everlasting arms.

Let us go forth with the watchword of Elisha, when his master had disappeared from his view, but his master's God still remained, crying, "Where now is the LORD, the God of Elijah?"

(2 Kings 2:14), and we will find that for all our need and work, Jesus Christ is "the same yesterday and today and forever" (Hebrews 13:8).

CHAPTER 14

Elisha

Lessons in Practical Faith

When they had crossed, Elijah said to Elisha, "Tell me, what can I do for you before I am taken from you?"

"Let me inherit a double portion of your spirit," Elisha replied. (2 Kings 2:9)

The life of Elisha differs from Elijah as the lightning which cleaves the sky differs from the light that illumines all the heaven, or as the tempests of November differ from the dawn of spring with its gentler and yet mightier forces. It is difficult for the ordinary mind to associate the same degree of power with the quiet and un-demonstrative forces of nature as with those that are more destructive and startling, but there is really more power in a single ray of sunlight than in a flash of lightning, and more divine potency in the gentle and peaceful dawn of morning or of springtide, than in a whole night of tempest or a winter of stormy elements. A child can destroy in

an hour the city which a generation or a century
has built. God's mightiest forces move on velvet
feet and with noiseless tread. God's greatest
temples rise in silence without even the noise of
the hammer or the jar of confusion. Such was the
special character of Elisha's work.

Elisha's Call

It is a beautiful lesson of prompt and obedient
faith. Returning from Horeb to Samaria, along the
valley east of the Jordan, Elijah halted at the little
village of Abel Meholah at the farm of the village
judge, Shaphat. Crossing over to the field in which
Shaphat's son was superintending the plowing
with 12 yoke of oxen, the old prophet suddenly approached Elisha, and, by an act which was understood to be a formal call to the prophetic office, he
threw his sheepskin mantle over his shoulders.
Elisha understood it immediately, but as he looked
at the stern figure of his master and thought of all
it meant to follow Elijah, he shrank for a moment
from instant obedience, and asked a brief interval
to take his farewell of his father's house. The old
prophet quickly answered, "Go back . . . What
have I done to you?" (1 Kings 19:20). This might
be interpreted to mean that there was no objection
in connection with the call which had been given
to so reasonable a request. More probably, however, it seems to mean that there was danger that
the gentle heart of Elisha might be unduly
weakened by the tender parting, and like the
young men that Christ called and rejected because

they put their domestic feelings and affections between Him and their work, that he too might need
to be guarded against the snare, even of the most
innocent attachments in connection with such a
call. So Elijah's answer rather seems to mean,
"You may go back if you wish. I am not compelling you to this service. I will excuse you if your
heart chooses something else."

Whatever the language meant, its effect was
most salutary, for Elisha made his parting brief
and prompt, and lest his business should be a
snare to him, he took the oxen with which he had
been plowing and the plow handles which he had
used, and turned them into a blazing sacrifice offered first to the Lord and then given to his servants as a parting feast. Then he passed on with
Elijah and henceforth became known as his servant: "Elisha . . . used to pour water on the hands
of Elijah" (2 Kings 3:11).

What a beautiful lesson of prompt decision and
humble consecration! Happy are they who as instantly obey, and who as wholly burn the last
bridge behind them! How many of us, alas, have
lost or lessened our life work by a faltering faith
or a divided life.

Elisha's Baptism for His Work

Elijah's ministry was drawing to a close. The
hour had come when he was to be translated to
his reward and his work committed to his follower. Elisha had a deep premonition that a crisis
was at hand and clung to his old master with the

tenderness of a child who feels that the hour of orphanage is near. The same message had come to the sons of the prophets also, and as they repeated it to Elisha he bid them to hold their peace, for he knew it too well and could not bear to speak of it. Something told him that it meant much to him of blessing and service, and he clung closely to Elijah and watched with him that one hour, as the disciples should have done in the garden with their departing Lord.

To each of us there comes such an hour of crisis. There are times in every life on which all our future hinges, when the Holy Spirit holds us close in the vigil of faith and prayer at the feet of Jesus, and we feel that we may not break the sacred spell or miss anything of the blessing which is waiting for our faith to claim. Elijah tested his disciple more than once to see if there was any weakness in his spirit or any willingness to return, but he met the one uncompromising answer, "As surely as the LORD lives, . . . I will not leave you" (2:4).

At length the great opportunity came: "Tell me, what can I do for you before I am taken from you?" (2:9). Then it was that Elisha's faith was proved; how much will he dare to ask? There was no hesitation; there was but one thing upon which his heart was wholly set, "Let me inherit a double portion of your spirit" (2:9). This did not mean more power and anointing than Elijah had possessed, but it was the Hebrew expression of the firstborn's full inheritance. This was truly given him. He inherited the ministry of his master, and with his spirit and power, there was more of the spirit of sonship and filial nearness to God than we find in any other character of the Old Testament. His whole spirit and life anticipated the grace and nearness of the gospel age.

But even this great request was not granted without a very searching test of Elisha's faith. Not unconditionally was the promise given: "If you see me when I am taken from you, it will be yours—otherwise not" (2:10) was the prophet's answer. And so Elisha was kept with his whole spirit intent on his master's movements. It was one of those crisis hours like that of Gethsemane, of which Jesus said to His disciples, "Could you men not keep watch with me for one hour?" (Matthew 26:40).

There are times in life when the whole being is absorbed in the duty of waiting on the Lord, and we feel that the whole future hangs upon the steadfast gaze and grasp of faith. And so Elisha clung to Elijah with persistent, inseparable love. From Gilgal to Bethel, from Bethel to Jericho, from Jericho to Jordan, he clung closer and closer to his side, walking on in silence under the strange spell of an unutterable expectancy.

At length the moment came, too sublime for any attempt of human rhetoric to describe, quiet and simple, no doubt, as God's greatest movements ever are. Perhaps there was a sudden flash of heavenly light in the midst of which appeared the chariots of God and the horsemen of fire, and a moment later, Elijah, transfigured into the likeness of their glory, dropped his mantle and passed out of sight before the steadfast gaze of his servant as he cried, "My father! My father! The chariots and horsemen of Israel!" (2 Kings 2:12). Then he lifted up the mantle of Elijah and rending his own clothes, put on the emblem of his master's spirit and stepped out in faith to use the supernatural enduement which had just fallen upon his spirit. He seized the mantle, and, stepping down again to the brink of the Jordan, smote the waters and they parted asunder as before, while he passed over to the sons of the prophets at Jericho, crying as the waves divided, "Where now is the LORD, the God of Elijah?" (2:14). As he met them again, the prophetic company could not fail to notice on his countenance the new glory of his baptism, and they cried, "The spirit of Elijah is resting on Elisha" (2:15).

We cannot fail to notice in Elisha's whole action the bold steppings of consistent faith. Had he failed in one of these steppings, it is doubtful if the blessing would have been complete. It was necessary that he should keep his eyes steadfastly fixed upon his master and witness his translation as the condition of his receiving his spirit. This is a fine illustration of the attitude of our faith with regard to our ascended Lord; it is as we keep our eyes fixed upon Him that we are transformed into His glory. But still further, Elisha must not only use the falling mantle but he must take it and rend his garments as he put it on. So we must take the enrobing power of the Spirit which Christ has left and put off our robes in exchange, ceasing from our strength and wisdom and going forth in the name of the Lord Jesus. Not only so, but he must step out and boldly use his blessing, and so he stepped down into the Jordan and bid its waters part asunder before Elijah's mantle, even as we must go forth expecting the power of the Spirit to accompany us and accomplish the work which we undertake in the name of Jesus. This is the cooperating attitude of faith, and it is to this that the victory is given. We are not to wait for some stupendous manifestation before we venture to use the power of God, but in blind obedience we must go forth and expect the waters to divide, the mountains to dissolve, the hearts of men to melt and break and the power of God to follow our words and acts.

Elisha's Life of Practical Faith

The prophet entered upon his unexampled career of service for his God and his country. It is a broad and beautiful illustration of the life of faith in all its fullness.

It illustrates preeminently the wide range of faith in all the variety of life's changing circumstances. In this respect Elisha was wholly different from Elijah. The latter lived in a narrow path of special ministry; the former filled a whole sphere of human experience. Elijah was like the zigzag lightning which strikes along a narrow path through the heaven; Elisha, like the broad sunlight which covers all the earth and sky. He was a man who lived among the people in the most varied relations; his home was in the city and his companions were princes and kings as well as the common people. Sometimes we find him in his house in Samaria; sometimes marching with the armies of Israel and Judah as the counselor of their captains. More frequently probably he was engaged in traveling over the country on a wide circuit of prophetic ministry, visiting the schools of the prophets, instructing the people and elevating the spiritual life of the nation.

In the course of these journeys the wealthy lady of Shunem, a village 25 miles north of Samaria, having often observed him going to and from, invited him to share her hospitality and prepared for him the prophet's chamber which has become a proverb through all the centuries, and afterwards received from his hand, first in birth, and then in resurrection life, her beloved child. Again we find him at Carmel and then again at Gilgal and yet again in the seclusion of the banks of the Jordan helping the young prophets to build their rustic home in the thicket over the river.

He lived the life of the people in all its varied extremes; he was a man of the largest sympathies, linked with the very fibers of the nation's life, so that when he died, even the godless Jehoash, Israel's wicked king, came to weep over his death and to cry, "My father! My father! . . . The chariots and horsemen of Israel!" (13:14). His example teaches us, therefore, that faith has ample opportunity for its exercise in every lot, whether our circumstances are peculiar or commonplace. It can accompany us and qualify us for the home of wealth, the dwelling place of the poor, the place of the statesman, the march of the soldier or the retirement of the recluse.

More particularly we learn from Elisha's life that faith can meet the urgent needs of want, poverty and the circumstances of outward distress and indigence. One of his first miracles was to heal the barren land; and more than once in his later life he met the cry of poverty and distress by multiplying the widow's oil, or increasing the loaves of bread for a hundred men, or saving the starving camp by water, or turning the famine of Samaria into plenty. So still, faith can take us through the straits of poverty and open the treasury of pecuniary supply, or make the scant means of the poor become ample for many hungry mouths, and cause the heart of the widow and orphan to sing for joy.

Faith to defend and overcome in the face of dangers and enemies kept Elisha unafraid in the midst of peril and enabled him ever to realize the divine resources which guarded and surrounded him. When the Syrian cavalry encompassed him on every side and his servant cried, "Oh, my lord, what shall we do?" (6:15), Elisha needed only to ask the Lord to open his servant's eyes and immediately he beheld the mountain thickly covered with the chariots and horses of God's unseen encampments. Instead of fleeing from his enemies he calmly approached them, struck them powerless with temporary blindness and then led them at his mercy into Samaria, where, instead of allowing Jehoram to kill them, he feasted them like princes, and then opened their eyes and allowed them to see their helplessness and sent them back to their own country, so astonished at his power and magnanimity that they never returned to Israel.

So faith can still keep the eye of the suffering saint on his almighty Savior and carry him through every danger without dismay. So, often has it brought to God's beleaguered ones the wings of His protection in danger's threatening hour; foiling the pursuers of the persecuted saints, covering sometimes the army of the Covenanters in a shroud of mist that hid them from their enemies, stopping the mouths of lions for a Livingstone or an Amot in the wilds of Africa, or holding back the clubs of Polynesian savages from a Paton when it seemed as if nothing could save him from instant assassination, and making many grateful hearts sing with trembling wonder and praise.

> How are Thy servants blessed, O Lord!
> How sure is their defense!
> Eternal wisdom is their guide,
> Their help omnipotence.

Elisha's faith reached to the needs of the suffering body and claimed the healing power of God. It was he who sent the commander of Syria, proud Naaman, to wash in Jordan's flood seven times and go forth healed of his leprosy, and, with discerning wisdom, kept from even speaking to him personally until the miracle was over, lest Naaman should trust in Elisha rather than Elisha's God.

The lessons of Naaman's healing embody the immutable principles on which God ever acts in dispensing His health and strength. Not until the proud heart was humbled into implicit submission to God's word, willing to take the advice of his very slaves and to do just as the prophet had commanded to the least minutiae, did the healing come. Even then it did not come until the seven times had been fulfilled and faith had completed its full season of testing and obedience. When it came, it was with that humble, grateful consecration to the service of God, which divine healing ever brings, sending Naaman back to his country and his home to be a witness henceforth for Jehovah alone.

Elisha's faith triumphed even over death itself. Along with Elijah in the Old Testament and Peter and Paul in the New, he stands distinguished as one of that quartet who even defied the king of terrors, and in the name of Jehovah called back the spirit to its deserted temple, and brought back from the cold embrace of death the Shunammite woman's boy. To us it may not be given to raise the dead, but to us it is given to have the power of the resurrection life through fellowship with the Risen One in our own souls and bodies. We too are constantly brought into situations where no power less than that which raised Jesus from the dead will meet the emergencies of our lives.

The faith of Elisha claimed the supernatural working of God and expected His power in circumstances where even the laws of nature rendered the result improbable or impossible. The finest illustration of this is where one of the young students of his household on the banks of the Jordan suddenly lost his ax in the river and cried to his master in deep distress because it was borrowed. The prophet at once commanded him to cut a branch from a tree and throw it into the stream, and immediately the iron floated, in defiance of the laws of gravitation; so showing him and us that there are higher laws which counteract natural laws when God pleases. Just as the vital power in our arm allows us to raise it when the law of gravitation would make it fall, so the law of supernatural force is higher than any tendency of inert matter. God would have us know that His power can help us beyond the probabilities of human reasoning, and that there is no weight so heavy and no law so trifling but He is both able and willing to afford us His omniscient wisdom and omnipotent help. A pin is not too small to ask from God and a mountain is not too heavy for His arm to raise. Oftentimes a deliverance as trifling as the recovery of a lost ax is His chosen occasion to show His thoughtful love and to teach us to trust Him under all circumstances for every need of soul and body.

Elisha's faith could even claim deliverance where the sufferer himself was to blame for his trouble. Such was the case with Jehoshaphat in the calamity which befell his army, through the unhallowed alliance with the kings of Edom and Israel. On account of his going with the enemies of God, his army was overcome with lack of water. Then it was that the wicked king of Israel completely broke down in unbelief and despair while good Jehoshaphat thought immediately of turning to the Lord and called for a prophet. Elisha was providentially present and through his faith the allied armies were delivered. Rebuking the wicked king, he kindly responded to the appeal of Jehoshaphat, and in answer to his prayer, the following morning the valley was flooded with water, with the added promise of victory over the enemy which signally followed.

It is most cheering thus to know that although we err and bring upon ourselves many troubles that might have been easily averted, yet God does not forsake even His mistaken child, but on his humble repentance and supplication is ever ready both to pardon and deliver. Let us not give up our faith because we have perhaps stepped out of the path in which He would have led us. The Israelites did not follow Him when He called them into the Land of Promise, yet God did not desert them. But during the 40 years of their wandering He walked by their side bearing their backsliding with patient compassion and waiting to be gracious unto them when another generation should come. "In all their distress he too was distressed, and the angel of his presence saved them. . . . he lifted them up and carried them all the days of old" (Isaiah 63:9). Likewise, while our wanderings bring us many sorrows and lose us many blessings, yet to the heart which truly chooses Him He has graciously said, "Never will I leave you; never will I forsake you" (Hebrews 13:5), and the penitent backslider will always find His mercy to pardon and restore and even teach some higher lessons by the very faults and failures, whose bitterness he had learned by painful experience.

Elisha's Dying Faith and Testimony

At last the long and busy life was about to close. Unlike his great master, he passed out of life through the ordinary gates of exit; for his was a life typical of the ordinary lot of men, as Elijah's was of the extraordinary. His faith might easily have claimed exemption from his last illness and possibly even from death itself, but like his great Master, of whom he was the especial type, in all things he was made like unto his brethren, that he might teach us the faith that could glorify God both in life and death. And so we read of "the illness from which he died" (2 Kings 13:14). We can scarcely doubt that all that was evil and of the enemy in connection with his illness was eliminated by the power of God, for we find his faith in freest and fullest exercise, even on his dying couch. The most beautiful example of faith found in the whole story of his life is his last interview with Jehoash. Elisha held the king's hand as he shot the arrow of believing prayer through the window of his house and claimed deliverance from Syria with the winged shaft, and then he told the hesitating king to take up the arrows that were left and smite them upon the ground, expressive of his own cooperating faith. When the king failed to rise to the full measure of the opportunity, the prophet reproved his tardy and timid faith and told him how he had lost the fullness of his victory which he should have wholly claimed. We see the wings of faith still buoyant and triumphant above every difficulty and limitation and we cannot doubt that a faith so mighty could easily have claimed his own recovery. But his work was done and he only waited to give this last lesson of trust and this last promise of blessing and then pass from the scene of his finished life.

It is a beautiful picture of faith that even infirmity and approaching dissolution cannot subdue or even cloud, reminding us that the Christian's last hours may be his brightest and that the sublimest triumphs of his life should be in the face even of his foes. Have we not all seen such victories, in which the withering frame and the worn out forces of nature and the very frailty of the outward temple made it more transparent to the glory that was shining out from within, while the walls were crumbling into decay and the inward guest was fluttering for its flight to a brighter sphere? Of such a scene it may be truly said:

Is that a deathbed where a Christian dies?
Yes, but not his. 'Tis Death himself that
dies.

The Posthumous Fruit of Faith

Elisha was dead but the power of his life could
not die. It has been happily said

The actions of the just,
Smell sweet and blossom in the dust.

So literally was it fulfilled in Elisha's time. His
very bones were vital in their touch long after his
dust had been laid to rest in an honored grave.
One day a body was suddenly dropped into his
sepulcher in haste and the moment it touched his
bones it became instinct with life, and the corpse
sprang to its feet, living and moving in resurrection life. This is a beautiful type of the resurrection power of Elisha's great Antitype, the Son of
God, but also equally suggestive of the power
that lingers behind the departing believer and
makes it true, even after 60 centuries, of Abel and
such as he, "by faith he still speaks, even though
he is dead" (Hebrews 11:4).

Perhaps the largest fruition of all true lives is
after they have passed from their earthly sphere. If
Isaiah could only know today, as probably he does
know, the millions that have rejoiced in the messages which his own generation refused to hear
and for which at last he was cruelly sawn apart by
Manasseh, he would feel repaid a millionfold for

all the trials of his suffering life. If Paul could only know the consolation and hope that he has ministered to the countless generations who have marched along the pathway from the cross to the kingdom above, he would be willing to go through a thousand lives and a thousand deaths such as he endured for the blessing that has followed since his noble head rolled in the dust by the Ostian gate of Rome. And if the least of us could only anticipate the eternal issues that will probably spring from the humblest services of faith, we should only count our sacrifices and labors unspeakable heritages of honor and opportunity, and would cease to speak of trials and sacrifices for God.

The smallest grain of faith is a deathless and incorruptible germ, which will yet plant the heavens and cover the earth with harvest of imperishable glory. Lift up your head, beloved; the horizon is wider than the circle that you can see. We are living, we are suffering, we are laboring, we are trusting, for the ages upon ages yet to come! "Let us not become weary in doing good, for at the proper time we will reap a harvest if we do not give up" (Galatians 6:9). With tears of transport we will cry some day, "How great is your goodness, which you have stored up for those who fear you, which you bestow in the sight of men on those who take refuge in you" (Psalm 31:19).

CHAPTER 15

Habakkuk

Rejoicing in Faith

Though the fig tree does not bud
  and there are no grapes on the vines,
though the olive crop fails
  and the fields produce no food,
though there are no sheep in the pen
  and no cattle in the stalls,
yet I will rejoice in the LORD,
  I will be joyful in God my Savior.
The Sovereign LORD is my strength;
  he makes my feet like the feet of a deer,
  he enables me to go on the heights.
      (Habakkuk 3:17-19)

Habakkuk is the prophet of faith. The motto of his little poem might be appropriately taken from a little verse which stands in the center of his prophecy, "The righteous will live by his faith" (Habakkuk 2:4). This beautiful verse has become indeed the keynote of the gospel in a very emphatic manner. The greatest of the New

Testament epistles, the epistle to the Romans, is practically a commentary on this text which the apostle quotes in the very beginning of that letter as the keynote of all that follows, "The righteous will live by faith" (Romans 1:17).

When that glorious gospel was to be reclaimed in the later centuries from the errors of Roman Catholicism, it was the same glorious verse which the Holy Spirit flashed into the mind of Luther and which became in turn, through him, the keynote of the Reformation. As he was climbing up the steps of the Lateran Church at Rome with slow and weary penance, vainly hoping for sanctification through his tortures and penances, the Holy Spirit flashed this verse in on his soul with resistless power and sent him back to Wittenburg to proclaim it to the world as the watchword of an emancipated gospel.

So too, the author of the epistle to the Hebrews points his most precious lessons on faith, and his chapter concerning faith is the finest commentary upon it in all the sacred writings, with another quotation from Habakkuk,

> So do not throw away your confidence; . . .
> For in just a very little while,
> "He who is coming will come and will not
>   delay.
>   But my righteous one will live by faith.
> And if he shrinks back,
>   I will not be pleased with him."
>   (Hebrews 10:35, 37-38)

So, then the two greatest epistles of the New Testament and the most important religious movement of the ages were largely inspired by this ancient prophet of faith, who sang his sublime song of holy confidence in the darkest days of Judah's overthrow. With Habakkuk it was not a mere literary composition, but a deep personal experience. He was one of that little band of whom Jeremiah was the central figure who kept alive the holy flame of piety and hope in the last dark days which preceded the captivity. He was surrounded not only with personal danger but saw with deeper concern the overwhelming disasters that were gathering about his country and which all his affectionate warnings seemed powerless to avert. His patriotic soul was filled with anguish and almost with despair, until from the wild cries of anxious fear he became quieted on the watchtower of prayer and heard the voice of God and saw the vision of His coming glory and deliverance, until his faith rose to meet it and poured itself out in his closing song of triumphant victory over tribulation and despair.

The Questioning of Faith

He began with the bitter cry of disappointment and perplexity, "How long, O LORD, must I call for help, but you do not listen?" (Habakkuk 1:2). It was like a wail of despair. The very heaven seemed closed against him and God to have forgotten his distress. It was like the upbraiding of the disciples in the storm as they cried, "Teacher,

don't you care if we drown?" (Mark 4:38), or
Martha's wild outburst of reproach, "Lord, . . . if
you had been here, my brother would not have
died" (John 11:21), or Hezekiah's vain moan
before the prayer of faith was given him for his
healing.

So we all too often begin to pray, but let not
even such be discouraged; the chattering of the
swallow and the mourning dove may yet be
turned into the notes of the nightingale and the
lark. If we are going to mourn let us mourn into
the ear of God rather than the empty air or the
ears of others.

The Listening of Faith

"I will stand at my watch and station myself on
the ramparts; I will look to see what he will say to
me, and what answer I am to give to this complaint" (Habakkuk 2:1). At length he ceased his
restless cries and began to keep still and hearken
for the voice of God. He wisely thought that perhaps God might have something to say to him
and perhaps there might be something wrong on
his part which needed to be corrected. He was
willing to listen to the voice of heaven even
though it may be reproof. And so he ascended to
the watchtower of prayer to wait upon the Lord
and to get so far above the clouds and mists of
earth that he could see the light of heaven and be
removed from the discords of time.

This is the attitude of blessing; faith must listen
to God's voice if it would have anything to rest its

confidence upon. In order to hear His voice, it must get quiet and separate itself from the discordant and distracting influences around it; and in the deepest humility it must be willing to listen to whatever He may say, willing even to hear the word of humbling reproof and lie down in silence and contrition at His feet. Thus will it hear what Habakkuk heard, not reproof at all, but the message of tenderest love and glorious promise.

Have we thus become still and learned the lesson of God's voice or have we so much to say that we have no leisure to hear? Let us become silent and say, "I will listen to what God the LORD will say; he promises peace to his people, his saints" (Psalm 85:8).

The Waiting of Faith

The message that came to Habakkuk was not a reproof but a gracious promise, telling him of deliverance and blessing; sure deliverance that would certainly come and would not fail, and yet deliverance that would be long enough delayed to test his faith to the utmost and educate him to the fact that "it is good to wait quietly for the salvation of the LORD" (Lamentations 3:26). The vision was yet for an appointed time, but at the end it would speak and not lie. "Though it linger, wait for it; it will certainly come and will not delay" (Habakkuk 2:3).

It is a promise that prepares us for delays. There are two distinct words here used to imply a waiting; one means delay, but the other—

linger—means hopeless disappointment, a delay that waits too long. The former, he says, will come but the latter will not. It will not wait too long. There will be trials of faith and patience but there will be no permanent failure, nor will one moment elapse which could have been spared. The whole plan of God will be wrought out, and in perfect maturity the blessing will come in all its fullness.

One of the hardest lessons which faith has to learn is to wait and yet not cease to trust, to see God wait and yet to see that He is not delaying but maturing His plan, that the very days are ripening the fruit, like the summer sun of July and August which are only mellowing the harvest for which the husbandman tarries. There is really no time lost although there may be much elapse. Some things have their cycle in an hour and some in a century; but His plans will complete their cycle whether long or short. Both the tender annual which blossoms but for a season and dies and the Columbia aloe which develops in a century are true to their normal principle. Many of us desire to pluck our fruit in June rather than wait until October and so, of course, it is sour and immature; but God's purposes ripen slowly and fully, and faith waits while it tarries knowing "it will surely come, it will not tarry" (2:3, KJV).

It is a perfect rest to fully learn and wholly trust this glorious promise. We may know without a question that His purposes will be accomplished when we have fully committed our ways to Him and are walking in watchful obedience to His every prompting. This faith will give a calm and tranquil poise to the spirit and save us from the restless fret and the trying to do too much ourselves. "In quietness and trust is your strength" (Isaiah 30:15), and "the one who trusts will never be dismayed" (28:16). While cooperating with God in all that He clearly shows us that we should do, yet we will calmly commit all our way to Him, knowing that He is working. "Be still before the LORD and wait patiently for him; do not fret when men succeed in their ways, when they carry out their wicked schemes" (Psalm 37:7). This indeed is the rest of faith, and they who have found it are happy indeed!

This glorious promise given to Habakkuk had reference no doubt to the Babylonian captivity and the subsequent return under Joshua and Zerubbabel, so fully described in the book of Ezra and also in the prophecies of Haggai and Zechariah. Jeremiah had predicted the very time of this trial and deliverance, telling them that after 70 years they should be restored and that the calamities of these sad years should end, and it is to this fixed point that Habakkuk refers. When the time came, it was made apparent how certain the promise was. In the book of Daniel we see the working out of God's glorious purposes and promises. At the ripe time he put the spirit of prayer upon Daniel for three full weeks, and upon Cyrus also He laid the burden of His will, until that monarch was compelled to issue a decree, proclaiming to all his realm that the God of heaven commanded him to send back the scattered Jews who were willing to return to rebuild His house in Jerusalem. To the very year the promise was fulfilled, and although it tarried it did not tarry too long or miss its time. God could lay His commands upon an emperor and take away his sleep at night until he fulfilled His high commission. And so still He can move all the force of earth and heaven to accomplish His great plans and bring about His precious promises.

The apostle has applied this precious promise to the second coming of the Lord Jesus Christ. Beautifully has he said, in the exquisite shading of the original, "For in just a very little while, [O how little!] 'He who is coming will come and will not delay'" (Hebrews 10:37). The first coming was exactly on time, and so will the second be. It may seem to tarry and the very hour is not known to us, nor perhaps is it fixed in the heavens by the chronology of years but rather by the chronometer of fitness, but when the conditions are fulfilled and the church and the world ready, then will He appear, and all will feel that it is the very juncture of infinite wisdom and infinite fitness.

So also we may apply this precious promise to our own present circumstances and the promises of Christ as given to meet them. For God does speak to His children and calls them each by name, and His Word is an individual message for all His own. To each of us, as to Jacob at Bethel,

Joseph in prison and David in exile, the same promise is given on which hangs all our future career. But each of us must learn both to hope and quietly wait; it is this which forms the very crucible of character, and trains for the noblest services and lives. These waiting years are the most fruitful seasons of our experience, and the very exquisiteness of Christ's faithfulness and wisdom is seen in the grace with which He trains us to keep the balance both of expectation and of patience—not passive but not impulsive, earnestly longing but hastening unto His will, yet calmly resting in His perfect wisdom and love.

Faith Triumphing over Tribulation and Disappointment

"Though the fig tree does not bud and there are no grapes on the vines, though the olive crop fails and the fields produce no food, though there are no sheep in the pen and no cattle in the stalls, yet I will rejoice in the LORD, I will be joyful in God my Savior" (Habakkuk 3:17-18). We would naturally have looked for faith's recompense but instead we find apparent refusal and continued disappointment. But this is the very soil of faith; this is the very time for the song of triumph and the shout of victory. Like the rose of the Alps which blossoms amid the icy glaciers of the mountain top, or the strange sweet blossom of the Sahara which only opens its petals when the hurricane sweeps the fiery plain, or the song of the nightingale which is heard only in the midnight, so faith reaches its highest development amid the darkness and tempest, when all around seems even to forbid its brightest expectation. It is nothing to believe when we see the fulfillment of our promise; the only time for faith to live is when sight and sense afford no comfort and we rest our confidence on the naked word of promise. Then Habakkuk not only trusted but began to sing, and he closed his sublime poem with a heavenly chorus of praise with all the stringed instruments upon Shigionoth. He was wise to turn prophecy and poetry into praise. When the dark hour of trouble comes there is no remedy or antidote stronger than the very spirit of praise. It is very beautiful to notice that the only time our Savior sang, at least so far as we have any record, was on His way to Gethsemane. The first song of Paul's ministry was in the darkest hour of his life, when in the gloomy dungeon of Philippi the whole prospect of his great missionary campaign for the evangelization of Europe seemed blasted forever. Luther used to say, "When your troubles become too great for prayer, then begin to sing," and when his heart was too sad for anything else he always began to sing one of his noble hymns and invariably found victory in praise.

It is said that once an ingenious musician threatened to break down a bridge, which certain engineers were constructing, with a single note of his instrument. They laughed him to scorn, but in answer to their ridicule he sat down on the bank of the river and began to sweep the chords of his instrument; seeking the right one. At last he found it. Then he prolonged that single note until it began to pierce the vibrating air with its shrill monotony, and soon the iron framework of the mighty bridge commenced to quiver in strange sympathy with the chords of music, trembling more and more violently while the note was prolonged, until it seemed as though it would shake the solid mechanism into ruin, and even the workmen cried out with fear and their scorn was turned into earnest entreaties that he would stop the magic of his fatal music. It is true that there are certain subtle laws of sound and air which need only to be perfectly made to produce as potent an effect as the illumination of an entire room by the touch of a child's finger on the light switch. We at least know that there are heavenly notes which have power to break down walls of adamancy and dissolve mountains of difficulty. The song of Paul and Silas burst the fetters of the Philippian jail; the choir of Jehoshaphat put to flight the armies of the Ammonites; and the song of faith will disperse our adversaries and lift our sinking hearts into strength and victory.

Beloved, is it the dark hour with you?—the winter of barrenness and gloom? Oh, let us remember that it is God's chosen time for the education of faith, and that beneath the surface He conceals precious and untold harvest of fruit. It will not always be winter; it will not always be night. When the morning comes and spring spreads its verdant mantle over the barren field, then we will be glad that we did not disappoint our Father in the hour of testing, but that faith had already claimed and seen in the distance the glad fruition which sight now beholds.

But Habakkuk's song would have been impossible if it had not been preceded by Habakkuk's vision. Before the sublime notes of these closing verses came the sublime vision of the opening verses of the chapter: the glorious picture of Jehovah's coming in His march of victory for the salvation of His people, bidding all the elements of nature to be subservient to His glory; the forces of the dread pestilence and fire to fulfill His mandates and scatter His people's enemies like the shadow of night before the rising day. That glorious vision is still fulfilled in every manifestation of His providence and grace for His people's deliverance. It is when we thus behold Him that all other circumstances shrink into insignificance. A sight of Jesus in His power and glory scatters all our forces and peoples the most barren waste with forms of life and loveliness, making the desert to blossom as the rose. This is the remedy for discouragement; this is the support of faith; this lifts up the hands that hang down and confirms the feeble knees (Isaiah 35:3) and enables us, like Him, to endure the cross, despising the shame, and to "fix our eyes on Jesus, the author and perfecter of our faith" (Hebrews 12:2). "For our light and momentary troubles are achieving for us an eternal glory that far outweighs them all. So we fix our eyes not on what is seen, but on what is unseen. For what is seen is temporary, but what is unseen is eternal" (2 Corinthians 4:17-18).

CHAPTER 16

Jeremiah

Add to Your Faith Courage

*"Ah, Sovereign LORD," [Jeremiah] said, "I
do not know how to speak; I am only a child."*
*But the LORD said to [him], "Do not say 'I
am only a child.' You must go to everyone I
send you to and say whatever I command you.
Do not be afraid of them, for I am with you
and will rescue you," declares the LORD.
(Jeremiah 1:6-8).*

The received canon of the Holy Scriptures
fails to present an adequate impression of
the place occupied by Jeremiah among the Old
Testament prophets in the estimation of his own
countrymen and the age which immediately followed his life. In the old Hebrew catalogs it
stands before Isaiah among the major prophets
and its author occupies the prominent place of affection and honor in their traditions and feelings.
His setting sun left a larger and longer twilight
than any other of the sacred characters. He was

regarded as the peculiar patron saint of Judea and Jerusalem. His spirit was supposed to hover over the nation in guardian love. He was said to have hidden the ark and the vessels of the sanctuary in the clefts of Mount Sinai, whence he is to restore them at the coming of the Messiah, and he was expected to appear again in the latter days of his country's history as the messenger of hope and blessing.

So strong was this expectation that in the days of our Lord, in answer to the inquiry, "Who do people say the Son of Man is?" the natural reply was, "Some say . . . Jeremiah" (Matthew 16:13-14). The halo left behind a departing life is a reasonable intimation of the magnitude of the life itself, and it is needless to say that such an influence was left upon the hearts of Jeremiah's people by no ordinary life and character.

Jeremiah indeed was worthy of their remembrance and gratitude, although while he lived he was the victim of their bitter oppositions and persecutions, and perhaps at last perished by their wicked and bloody hands. The story of his life is full of vivid incidents all woven into the whole fiber of his prophetic writings. We know it in greater minutiae of detail than in the case of any other of the later prophets of Judah. Moreover it has the plaintive charm of sorrow; it was all cast in the mold of suffering and every message draws intense interest from the personal events which formed the framework of his life. It was peculiarly a life of faith, a faith which developed unusual lines of suffering and service, especially of courageous achievement and endurance.

Faith Reaches the Supernatural

Faith always reaches the supernatural, and then usually leads above the natural and often contrary to it. In Jeremiah's natural temperament there was nothing that fitted him for the peculiar work to which he was called, but everything was wholly out of harmony with his life and calling. He was sensitive, shrinking, timid and weak, naturally recoiling from harshness and severity, shrinking from self-assertion and aggressiveness, fitted rather to sympathize with and comfort the sorrowing than rebuke the proud and defy the powers of evil. When the first message came to him sending him forth to his strange work, he cried in agony, "I do not know how to speak; I am only a child" (Jeremiah 1:6). Yet it was this weak, shrinking man whom God especially chose to hurl the thunderbolts of His judgment against the princes, the priests and the people of the land, and to stand like a wall of adamancy against the surges of their furious opposition. God did not need his natural strength; had he been constitutionally aggressive and vindictive, his words would have been the fierce utterances of passion and would have had no heavenly power. It was the fact that they were contrary to his natural feeling and instincts that made them more terribly the messages of

God and the warnings of His holy indignation.
God taught him that He could become his utterance and power; by touching the prophet's
mouth with His burning hand, he was instantly
clothed with heavenly fire and endued with the
power of the Holy Spirit. "You must go to
everyone I send you to and say whatever I command you. . . . Now, I have put my words in
your mouth" (1:7, 9).

Even still, faith can anoint the weakest instrument with heavenly power and clothe the stam-
mering tongue with effective utterance and
resistless eloquence if we are but willing, like
Jeremiah, to go where He bids and speak what
He gives. So let us be willing to speak as the
oracles of God and prophesy according to the
proportion of faith.

Not only was Jeremiah naturally unfitted for his
work but the work was most distressing to him.
Could he have but comforted his people and
spoken to them the messages of promise, his
heart would have sung for joy, but his one consuming message was reproof, warning and impending judgment. Again and again he felt he
would tell it no more, but he adds, "his word is in
my heart like a fire, a fire shut up in my bones. I
am weary of holding it in; indeed, I cannot"
(20:9). And so for nearly half a century with the
gentlest of hearts and the tenderest love for his
people, he stood before them as the messenger of
God's terrors and the witness for His unsullied
honor and authority.

God still leads His children to unwelcome work and tasks from which every instinct of their nature shrinks. Gladly would we speak the honeyed words of comfort, but these would be false and deceptive, and deeper and deeper we must press the given decree to the heart, until proud self-will is slain and laid at the feet of the Lord in helplessness and confession. Then we can speak the words of comfort which will not deceive. True faith will accept whatever task the Master gives, satisfied if He is glorified. Such was the ministry of Isaiah to his own countrymen. "Go and tell this people: 'Be ever hearing, but never understanding'" (Isaiah 6:9). Faithfulness, not always success, is the test of service. Ministries like Noah's, Isaiah's and Jeremiah's were but little more than protests against the unbelief of their times, chiefly spent with the mournful complaint, "Who has believed our message and to whom has the arm of the LORD been revealed?" (53:1). These ministries will yet have the highest recompense when all our actions are weighed in the measure of faith and the scale of divine judgment.

No Courage but Still Brave

In the natural Jeremiah had no courage, but actually he was the bravest of men. His life was wholly spent in the midst of peril, persecution and exposure, even death itself. Again and again he was required to do the most daring things in the face of his enemies: sometimes to stand in the midst of the multitude and proclaim the approaching judgments of God; sometimes to confront the popular and tin-serving prophets of the temple and expose their falsehoods and contradict their rose-colored promises of coming blessings; sometimes to protest single-handedly against the course of action upon which the king and the princes and all the people had decided and to warn them of destruction and ruin if they persisted in it; sometimes to stand in the temple court and announce amid the horror of the hearers and their cries of blasphemy, that Jerusalem should be plowed as an heap; sometimes to take a position which exposed him to the charge that he was disloyal to his country, that he was weakening the hearts of the people by his discouraging messages and inviting sure defeat from their enemies by the spirit of depression he threw over them by his words. Sometimes he had to go and stand before the king and read the scathing words which Jehovah had revealed, unfolding His coming judgments upon the wicked Jehoiakim, and more than once to find himself instantly arrested by a furious mob and about to be put to immediate death as a traitor to his country.

All this the shrinking, gentle Jeremiah had to face. And all this he did face, again and again, with calm, unfaltering front for years—almost half a century—never once seeking to save his life, but wholly concerned for the honor of God and the welfare of his country.

From where did this sublime courage, so much more lasting than natural impetuosity and passion's fire, come? Ah, it was the courage of faith. The secret of it is given in the first chapter of his book. "Do not be terrified by them" (Jeremiah 1:17), was the stern message of God when He called and anointed Jeremiah. "Get yourself ready! . . . Do not be terrified by them, or I will terrify you before them" (1:17). The one foe he was to fear was fear itself; the one peril that would confound and destroy Jeremiah was a timid front. And so he set his face like a flint in the presence of God, fearing nothing but disobedience to Jehovah. God panoplied him with His own gracious might and made him, as He explains it in His own promise, "a fortified city, an iron pillar and a bronze wall to stand against the whole land" (1:18).

So still He gives us His courage too. True fortitude is not mere human daring, but the heart of Christ given to His own depending child, the faith and courage of the son of God put on as a breastplate of heavenly armor. The Word doesn't say "add to yourself," but "add to your faith" (2 Peter 1:5).

It is most beautiful to observe how God honored the courage of faith by granting His almighty protection and bringing Jeremiah safely through the perils under which his cowardly contemporaries perished. There are no two characters more strongly marked than Jeremiah and Zedekiah; the one is the brave and resolute prophet and the other the vacillating and irresolute king. Again and again did Zedekiah send for Jeremiah and beg for counsel from Jehovah, and faithfully and most graciously was the council given. It was not inevitable that Jerusalem should fall or Zedekiah perish. Again and again he was told that if he would be obedient to Jehovah he and his people would be safe, but his timid answer was always, "I am afraid of the Jews" (Jeremiah 38:19). He did not have the courage to carry out the prophet's instructions and the Lord's commands.

And what was the result? Tighter and tighter grew the coils around the doomed city. At last its destruction was inevitable. Then the timid king, seeing the capture of Jerusalem to be at hand, with cowardly selfishness, made a last bid for his own safety. Fleeing with a small detachment of his house and army through one of the most obscure gates of the city, he escaped beyond the lines of the Chaldeans in the night and almost reached the shelter of the land of Moab. But he was immediately detected and pursued by Nebuchadnezzar's army, captured before morning, brought before the king at Riblah, and treated with the most refined cruelty and severity. With a chain through his nose he was dragged before the king while Nebuchadnezzar held the chain and Zedekiah knelt prostrate at his feet with hands and face lifted up in a pitiful supplication. His own sons were brought in and one by one slain before his eyes; and then, with the fearful sight fresh upon the burning eyeballs and deeply engraved on the tablets of memory, a spear was lifted by the king's rude hand and instantly dashed into Zedekiah's own eyes. As his sight went out in darkness and agony, the hideous vision was stereotyped forever on his brain. Then he was hurled in a cage like a chained beast, carried off to Babylon and confined in a dungeon until his death, without a single ray of joy or hope ever to light up his gloom. This was the recompense of fear.

Others Rise to His Defense

But now let us look at Jeremiah. Appearing in the temple court with one of his daring messages, he was instantly seized by one of the princes who immediately determined upon his death. Without attempting to escape he fearlessly declared, "As for me, I am in your hands; do with me whatever you think is good and right. Be assured, however, that if you put me to death, you will bring the guilt of innocent blood on yourselves" (26:14-15). Then it was that his brave stand aroused the sympathy of some in the crowd, and one began to tell how Hezekiah listened to the message of Micah and repented and averted the judgments. Another told of Urijah who in the days of Jehoiakim had spoken such brave words as Jeremiah, but upon the king's displeasure had fled to Egypt, and how the king had sent to Egypt and brought him back and slain him, and in contrast, Jeremiah's character only excited their admiration. And so voice after voice was raised for the brave prophet and the counsels of his friends prevailed and his life was saved. The dark and desperate hour of ruin came; he made no attempt to escape from the gathering storm. He remained in Jerusalem, true to his people to the last, and when the city fell he seemed to have been the only man that was not harmed.

The very first thing the captains of Nebuchadnezzar's army did was to find him out by the express orders of the king and see that he was guarded from danger and injury. And when the city was to be dismantled and its people carried captive, he was offered the honorable alternative of remaining with them or going forth in freedom and honor into Babylon under the royal protection of Nebuchadnezzar. The only man that was not afraid was unharmed and treated like a prince, while those who sought their own lives and interests miserably perished. How safe, how happy they who trust Jehovah!

> Fear Him, ye saints, and then ye shall
> Have nothing else to fear,
> Make you His service your delight,
> Your wants shall be His care.

Endurance Born of Faith

There is a kind of endurance very different from that which faces the sudden peril of the foe, a patience that suffers long and endures unto the end; and this too is born of faith. Jeremiah was a great sufferer; he is called "the weeping prophet." "I am the man who has seen affliction" (Lamentations 3:1) was his own complaint. As the very type of the suffering Son of Man he could say, "Look around and see. Is any suffering like my suffering that was inflicted on me, . . . in the day of his fierce anger?" (1:12). It was the kind of suffering that had no consciousness of personal punishment in it. It was suffering largely for the sake of others.

Much of our suffering comes from this cause, and the faith that sustained the mourning prophet can be our stay and consolation. Part of his suffering consisted of personal hardship and persecution. Much of his time was spent in imprisonment. And he has told us the circumstances of his dungeon life, immured in a deep pit, whose bottom was thick with mire and filth so that his feet sank down in the mire and he was almost drowned in the vile and horrible dungeon, rescued only by the faithfulness of a Cushite who drew him up with cords out of the horrible pit.

But his deepest sufferings were on account of the sins and prospects of his people.

> Since my people are crushed, I am crushed;
>   I mourn, and horror grips me.
> Is there no balm in Gilead?
>   Is there no physician there?
> Why then is there no healing
>   for the wound of my people?
> Oh, that my head were a spring of water
>   and my eyes a fountain of tears!

I would weep day and night
　　for the slain of my people.
　　(Jeremiah 8:21-9:1)

To see those he loves sinning, suffering and madly rushing to destruction is ever a deep and bitter agony in the truehearted child of God. Nothing but the highest faith in the wisdom, mercy and faithfulness of God can sustain us in such distracting grief. From all human sources Jeremiah turned to God alone for comfort and he tells us the sources of his comfort.

> "Cursed is the one who trusts in man,
> 　who depends on flesh for his strength
> 　and whose heart turns away from the
> 　　LORD.
> He will be like a bush in the wastelands;
> 　he will not see prosperity when it comes.
> He will dwell in the parched places of the
> 　　desert,
> 　in a salt land where no one lives.
> "But blessed is the man who trusts in the
> 　　LORD,
> 　whose confidence is in him.
> He will be like a tree planted by the water
> 　that sends out its roots by the stream.
> It does not fear when heat comes;
> 　its leaves are always green.
> It has no worries in a year of drought
> 　and never fails to bear fruit." (17:5-8)

God Himself was the source of Jeremiah's comfort, and in His presence he was lifted above the
consequences of many of the terrible effects of
the conduct of those about him. And so in his
sorrowful book of Lamentations he says,

> Because of the LORD's great love we are
>   not consumed,
>   for his compassions never fail.
> They are new every morning;
>   great is your faithfulness.
>
> The LORD is good to those whose hope is
>   in him,
>   to the one who seeks him;
> it is good to wait quietly
>   for the salvation of the LORD.
>
> For he does not willingly bring affliction
>   or grief to the children of men.
>
> Why should any living man complain
>   when punished for his sins?
> Let us examine our ways and test them,
>   and let us return to the LORD.
>   (Lamentations 3:22-23, 25-26, 33, 39-40)

We see that this suffering fellow-traveler has
tasted not only the hard places of our journey but
the fountains and sheltering valleys, too, and left
many a draught for travelers to drink and quench
their thirst as they follow him.

A Ministry of Love

While Jeremiah's ministry was largely one of rebuke and reproof, it was preeminently one of love. We are never qualified to try reproof until we do it with a breaking heart; so all his messages of judgment were quenched in tears. It was love for his people that won their grateful homage when he passed away. Misunderstood by his own generation, the heart of the succeeding ages met and went out to greet the great heart that brooded over them in the darkest hour of their need. Such was the spirit of Jeremiah's life; he hovered over Jerusalem like a guardian spirit, like a mother's heart, anticipating every day the slow and certain doom that was advancing to meet them, and yet determined to do his best to avert it, or if that could not be done, to suffer with them. Oh, there is no love so tender as that which can love on in the face of refusal and rejection! In this respect Jeremiah was the type of Him who wept over Jerusalem, who said, "Father, forgive them, for they do not know what they are doing" (Luke 23:34). But such love is born of faith. Natural passion will not love like this, but the love that comes from the fountain of Christ's heart and which goes out to others because He bids us love them never fails.

So Jeremiah loved Israel. They were God's people and God had made them his and he loved them with a love as strong as death. When they refused to hear him he still pleaded; when he saw them about to suffer the horrors which he had predicted, he longed to share them without one upbraiding voice. When he was offered the privilege of honorably escaping from their midst he refused to go, but still chose to abide among his own people to live and die. When they came to consult him about going down into Egypt, he warned them against going, but when they persisted in going he went with them, and when he still continued to warn and teach them they at last, it is said, sealed his faithful lips with his own blood, and he gave up to them his very life as the last and highest pledge of love.

So Jesus has loved us, and so we can love sinful men and unworthy hearts in the faith that works by love that

> Bears and forbears and will not tire,
> Like Stephen's an unquenched fire.

Faith That Looks Beyond the Present

Jeremiah has given us the very finest illustration of the faith that looks beyond the present and in the darkest hour counts upon the certainty of the future and calls the "things that are not as though they were" (Romans 4:17). When Jerusalem was encompassed with armies and the villages around were occupied by the enemy, so that real estate was valueless and the future prospects of houses and lands were at the lowest ebb, it was then that with that sublime audacity possible only to a man that believes in God, he publicly invested his money in purchasing his ancestral estate in the village of Anathoth, subscribing the evidences and sealing the transaction by every formality of law. This proclaimed in the name of the Lord that he did this as a pledge to the people that, notwithstanding the dark circumstances around them, houses and fields should yet be possessed in the land, for a bright and glorious day of restoration and deliverance was about to come when the time of chastening will have passed and the era of promise have come again. It was a beautiful symbol of practical faith. It was based upon his own prophetic word that after 70 years the captivity of Judah should be accomplished and the scattered tribes should return to Jerusalem. And grandly it was fulfilled to the letter and the year, so grandly and signally that even the mightiest king on earth, proud heathen Cyrus, was compelled to fulfill the vision of Jeremiah, by making a public decree, declaring that Jehovah had bidden him rebuild Jerusalem and invite her captive children to return to their native home. So Jeremiah's audacity was vindicated and Jehovah's prophecy gloriously fulfilled, as faith ever will be honored.

Oh, for the faith that in the dark present and the darker future will dare to subscribe the evidences and seal up the documents for the time of waiting and then begin to testify to the certainty of its hope like the prophet of Anathoth! The word Anathoth had a beautiful meaning: "echoes." So faith is the "echo" of God and God always gives the "echo" to faith, as He answers it back in glorious fulfillment. Oh, let our faith echo also the brave claim of the ancient prophet and take our full inheritance with his glorious shout, "Ah, Sovereign LORD. . . . Nothing is too hard for you" (Jeremiah 32:17). And back like an echo will come the heavenly answer to our hearts. "I am the LORD, the God of all mankind. Is anything too hard for me?" (32:27). "This is what the LORD says: . . . 'Call to me and I will answer you and tell you great and unsearchable things you do not know' " (33:2-3).

The highest reach and sublimest honor of Jeremiah's faith was that he discerned amid the failure of earthly kings and priest and prophets the form of the coming King and the grace and glory of His first and second advent. He saw the first covenant broken, but above its ruins rose the promise which is the very foundation of all our gospel privileges.

> "I will make a new covenant
> with the house of Israel . . .
>   after that time," declares the LORD.
> "I will put my law in their minds
>   and write it on their hearts.
> I will be their God,
>   and they will be my people." (31:31, 33)

> "I will inspire them to fear me, so that they
> will never turn away from me. I will rejoice
> in doing them good and will assuredly plant

them in this land with all my heart and soul." (32:40-41)

It was Jeremiah who saw and revealed the glorious truth of Christ our Righteousness, and the deep mystery of our union with Him in a bond so close that His righteousness becomes ours and His name also, as the Bridegroom's name is named upon His Bride. "In his days Judah will be saved and Israel will live in safety. This is the name by which he will be called: The LORD Our Righteousness" (23:6). This is his picture of the glorious Bridegroom. But later comes the picture of the Bride and her transcendent name, "In those days Judah will be saved and Jerusalem will live in safety. This is the name by which it will be called: The LORD Our Righteousness" (33:16). She bears His very name, the very name of His righteousness. In Him she has divine righteousness itself, for the Bride is lost in her husband and all that is His is hers. Glorious prophet! Glorious vision! Glorious gift of righteousness and honor which we inherit! Israel little knows how much their prophet brought them. Their eyes will yet weep as bitterly as his have wept when they awake to see how much their unbelief has lost of the inheritance of his prophetic vision and his faithful life.

So for us, let faith ever rise from human failures to the unfailing faithfulness and righteousness of Christ. Oh, it is not until all is dead as ashes around us that we know all the meaning of His sufficiency and grace!

CHAPTER 17

Daniel

The Purpose, the Proving, the Prayer and the Promise of Faith

*But Daniel resolved not to defile himself . . .
(Daniel 1:8)*

*During the night the mystery was revealed to
Daniel in a vision. Then Daniel praised the
God of heaven. . . . Then King Nebuchadnezzar fell prostrate before Daniel and paid him
honor and ordered that an offering and incense
be presented to him. The king said to Daniel,
"Surely your God is the God of gods." (Daniel
2:19, 46-47)*

God sometimes chooses a single individual to
accomplish, for His glory, the purpose
which a whole nation had failed to fulfill. This
was peculiarly true in the case of Daniel.
Jerusalem had failed as a witness for God among
the nations, and through her own faithlessness
had become a public reproach to the name of

213

Jehovah, until she had to be humiliated and destroyed for the vindication of His own honor and word. Then He chose a single Hebrew captive to accomplish, in the face of the world, the purpose to which she had proved faithless. By his simple faith and steadfast fidelity, Daniel became the instrument of vindicating Jehovah's name before the nations and bringing the proud monarch of the world, the very destroyer of Jerusalem, to acknowledge and submit to the God of Israel and glorify His name above all gods.

Looking at his life from a human standpoint, men might naturally have thought of him rather in connection with his prominent position as a statesman and his splendid services for the empires of Babylon and Persia. But looking at Daniel from the standpoint of revelation, the Holy Spirit sees chiefly his spirit of faith, and the one record gathered out of his life by the author of the epistle to the Hebrews is the single passage which refers to his confidence in God and the faith by which he stopped the mouths of lions (11:33). The Old Testament narrative echoes the same thought as it tells us that "no wound was found on him, because he had trusted in his God" (Daniel 6:23). The secret, therefore, of Daniel's character and the key to his life was faith.

The Purpose of Faith

In the very beginning of the book, the keynote of his character is sounded. "Daniel resolved not

to defile himself with the royal food and wine"
(1:8). This was a very decided determination; he
had quite made up his mind to act on a certain
principle of self-denial and simplicity of life and
he inflexibly adhered to his purpose. Decision of
character is the very ground and soil of faith. The
will in man is the point of contact through which
God acts upon us, and, like the helm and engine
of the vessel, it is the directing and impelling
power of life. Without a strong purpose, faith is
impossible. They greatly err who look for its
sphere in the emotions. Its seat is in the will. A
clear, calm, inflexible choice is the mightiest element in the life of faith. God is always looking for
men on whom He can depend to take a firm
stand and maintain it. Some souls are like the jel-
lyfish and would not stand the strain of God's
blessings or testings; or, to change the figure, like
a towrope which would snap under the first pull
of the engine, in contrast with the chain cable
which attaches the tugboat to the vessel as it pulls
her over the bar or holds the anchor which fixes
her securely in the face of the storm. God can
carry us through anything if we have fiber
enough to stand the pull.

The other day a company of workmen were
preparing to rear aloft some heavy ornamental
stones in the front of one of our new buildings.
Instead, however, of going to work to raise the
stone, one of them stepped out into the middle of
the street and began to dig up a piece of granite
pavement. What was he going to do with the

rough and ordinary stone? Surely not place it among the handsome blocks of the elaborate facade. It was soon evident what he intended in digging out the stone. He drove a heavy crowbar many feet into the solid ground and then tightly wedged it among the granite blocks of the pavement. Then he fastened a strong cable to it and attached it to the pulleys of the derrick and began to hoist the handsome blocks of cut stone into their places on the wall. Ah! It was easy to understand now what it meant. He needed a fixed anchorage for his machinery that would beat the strain of the heavy masses that were to be raised aloft, and this had to be made secure and firm before a block could be hoisted to the building.

God, too, is building His beautiful and costly temples, and many a polished stone does He want to place in the finished structure of our sanctified lives, but before He can do so, He too must have an anchorage that will hold. He sometimes spends months and years in driving a little peg in the ground and securing a fastening for His promises in our faith and will. Therefore, He generally trains us to firmness of purpose and fixedness of choice in a thousand little things, which in themselves may be of no moment, but are indispensable as lessons in the school of faith. And when He has found a man that will stand firm wherever he has planted his feet in conviction and will keep faith with God no matter what it costs, there is nothing that He cannot and will not do for such a soul. With delight He says of men like this, as He said of Abraham, "I have chosen him, so that he will direct his children and his household after him . . . so that the LORD will bring about for Abraham what he has promised him" (Genesis 18:19).

Beloved, have we learned the lessons of the primary school of faith? Have we accustomed ourselves always to act from conviction, to stand inexorably as the granite rock and to purpose in our hearts like Daniel with a determination which earth and hell cannot shake?

Such spirits are the chosen vessels for divine grace and victorious faith. And it is worth a lifetime of waiting to have learned this lesson thoroughly and be able, when God bids us, to stand firm even at the cost of life itself. Sometimes God tests us, as He did Daniel, about our bodies. There are men and women whose highest discipline in the life of faith has come in the determination that they will trust only God for the care of their bodies, and though others laugh as they suppose at their expense and ridicule their foibles and scruples, yet the power to stand in such a purpose is the key to a thousand victories in every other department of Christian life and work. Sometimes the purpose is proved in the determination to avoid alcohol or the indulgences of appetite as Daniel and his companions determined. There are many men and women whose characters and lives have been established and ennobled by the inflexible adherence of their youth to such a course of self-denial in the midst of the fascinations and temptations of society. It is not merely the immediate benefit derived from the abstinence, whether it be from drugs or indulgences, though that is very great, but it is the spiritual discipline and self-restraint and the power to stand.

The Proving of Faith

Great faith always involves great trials. The stronger the purpose of fidelity to God, the stronger the pressure the enemy will bring to bear. The great trial of Daniel's life at length came; he did not need to seek it, but simply to stand firm in his accustomed place of piety and consistency. He met the decree of Darius forbidding the worship of Jehovah and demanding an act of impious sacrilege by simply doing as he had been accustomed. There was no flourish of trumpets, no noisy display, but the calm consistent steadfastness of faith and duty. He was not any more demonstrative than usual in his piety, but as was his custom he went to his house and with his windows open toward Jerusalem he prayed to Jehovah "just as he had done before" (Daniel 6:10). There is an inexpressible sublimity in that phrase "just as he had done before." His was the attitude of inflexible fidelity that calmly chooses its course for the sake of principle and conscience, and then moves unswervingly on through evil report and good report, through prosperity or peril, acting each day and hour as scrupulously and faithfully as if it knew that tomorrow it had to stand before the Judge.

Daniel's faith did not avert the fearful ordeal, and God has not promised any of us that we will escape fiery trials. Daniel went into the den of lions and all the night long he stood face to face with their savage jaws and glaring eyes. And so we will pass through the waters and fires too, but the waters will not overflow us, nor will the fire kindle upon us. The lions were paralyzed by the hand of God, and "no wound was found on him, because he had trusted in his God" (6:23). There is no doubt but that in that fiery crisis he was enabled to claim victory over the fierce will of the ferocious creatures by his side, and that his safety was due to the attitude of victorious faith which he was enabled to maintain.

God has often enabled His suffering saints to rise above the passions of men and even the ferocity of beasts and to disarm the hate and power of hell by tranquil reliance upon the arm which restrains all other arms and controls all the fierce elements of earth and hell. God has revealed to us the great secret of faith as the key to all the forces of the universe. There is no peril so dreadful as the peril of fear, and there is no protection so sure as tranquil trust in God in the most trying and dangerous hour. "What I feared has come upon me" (Job 3:25) is the sad confession of Job. "Do not be terrified by them, or I will terrify you before them" (Jeremiah 1:17) was God's command to Jeremiah. "I sought the LORD, and he answered me; he delivered me from all my fears" (Psalm 34:4) is the psalmist's glorious testimony. And it is soon followed by another acknowledgment, "This poor man called, and the LORD heard him; he saved him out of all his troubles" (34:6).

Our first victory must always be over unbelief and anxiety. "God is within her, she will not fall; God will help her at break of day" (46:5). Will we look upon our trials, beloved, henceforth in God's light, not as calamities that have come to overwhelm us, but as tests sent to prove our faith; not as mountains thrown across our path to impede our progress, but as steps of ascension upon which we may mount to loftier heights? This is indeed God's philosophy of suffering. "Do not be surprised at the painful trial you are suffering, as though something strange were happening to you" (1 Peter 4:12). "These have come so that your faith—of greater worth than gold, which perishes even though refined by fire—may be proved genuine and may result in praise, glory and honor when Jesus Christ is revealed" (1:7). When the next difficulty crosses our path, let us remember that God is simply watching to see what we will do, whether we will yield to our forces and circumstances or honor Him by simply saying, "This is but a greater occasion for my Father's help, and I trust the more triumphantly and claim His help the more certainly and divinely." The greater the need the more worthy is it of His omnipotence and faithful love.

The faith of Daniel and its sublime victory accomplished more for the honor and glory of

Jehovah than all the centuries of Israel's history, compelling the proud Cyrus and the whole Persian empire to acknowledge the supremacy of Jehovah and to yield to the will of a single faithful man who would rather die than dishonor God. Thus, without stepping aside one hairbreadth from the path of duty, without preaching a sermon or writing a volume or building up a religious institution, but by being true to God a single man became the greatest witness for truth and God in all the last seven centuries of the old dispensation, and compelled the world to acknowledge the truth and the majesty of faith and righteousness.

We little know how much hangs upon our hours of trial and the simple question of saying "no" in the ordinary occurrences of life and solicitations of temptation. May God give us grace not to miss the blessing of our trials and the real fruition which they may bring to our Master's glory and our eternal usefulness.

The Prayer of Faith

Having been called and fully proved amid the trials of life, Daniel was next called to the higher ministry of believing prayer. Those who have proved God most thoroughly in the actual tests of life's difficulties will ever be found most ready to claim the largest things through the channels of prayer. There is no school of prayer so valuable as the school of sorrow. Having found God faithful to us in our own needs we can claim His promises for the help of others and the advancement of His own kingdom. The closing years of Daniel's life were largely given to communion with God. With all the cares of a complicated empire on his hands, he found ample time for long seasons of special prayer. The most remarkable of these examples is recorded in the ninth and 10th chapters of his prophecy. There we find him devoting a long season to special waiting upon God in fasting and prayer.

The peculiarity of this season of prayer was that it was wholly unselfish. The burden that he was carrying was not his own, but the sorrows and needs of others, the calamities of his people Israel, and the interests of God's kingdom in connection with their restoration. It is the most instructive chapter on prayer in the Bible and reveals some of the deepest principles of this profound mystery of communion with God. He had learned from the sacred volume that the time of a great promise was drawing near. The prophet Jeremiah had foretold, not only the sad captivity of Judah, but also the glad sequel, their future restoration after a period of 70 years. Daniel knew that this time had about expired, but instead of waiting supinely and passively to see what God would do, or saying "if He has promised there is no need of praying, for He will perform His word," he set himself all the more to plead with God and claim the fulfillment of His promise.

God would have us learn that even His surest promises must be endorsed by faith and presented by prayer at the heavenly bank that the name of Jesus is fulfilled, and the record go upon the books of God to the praise of His eternal faithfulness. The very fact that God had promised was the solid basis of his prayer, and so on our part the prayer of faith will always be based on the promises of God.

We also learn from Daniel's prayer that the moment we claim the promise of God in humble faith, our prayer is heard and answered. When the angel came with the message of heaven to the long entreating prophet he announced to him that from the very first day of his protracted season of prayer it was heard, and the answer was decreed and dispatched. There was no need, therefore, for Daniel's 21 days of crying unto God in order to make God hear and answer, for God heard and answered from the beginning, as He ever does the first cry of believing prayer. But there was no fault in the waiting and supplicating, nor is there any blame in our continuing in prayer and watching therein in fasting and supplication. The only thing to be guarded is that we be sure to believe from the beginning and continue waiting, not in suspense and doubt, but in thanksgiving listening for the Master's word.

Why then was not the answer immediately made manifest? Oh, here we learn some of the deep secrets of God's kingdom. "Twenty-one days ago," says the angel, "your prayer was heard and I was sent to help you. But all those 21 days I have been fighting my way to you through the ranks of hell. Forces, countless and infernal, have infested all the way and fought as demons to prevent the answer I have come to bring. The Prince of Persia withstood me these twenty-one days" (see Daniel 10:12-14). Who was the Prince of Persia? No doubt he was one of the principalities in heavenly places whom the god of this world sets over the different sections of his dark kingdom. We know the governments of this world are administered by the direction of the devil. Christ did not contradict him when Satan said of the kingdoms of this world "[they have] been given to me, and I can give [them] to anyone I want to" (Luke 4:6). Doubtless some spirit of superhuman wisdom and power is the special guardian of each particular section of his kingdom to work with his utmost power, with the aid of his innumerable emissaries, against the kingdom of God and for the injury and ruin of men.

Perhaps this Prince of Persia was the satanic spirit who specially reigned in the Persian policy that had opposed the purpose of Cyrus; perhaps trying to excite intestine wars and commotions that would preoccupy the mind of Cyrus and distract him from God's call; perhaps working directly upon his own mind to prevent his issuing the great decree for the restoration of the Jews; perhaps working against the Jews themselves in Persia. It doesn't matter how. It is enough that he resisted with all his might and that when Gabriel reached at length the river where Daniel knelt with the tidings of deliverance, the battle was not yet ended, but he was immediately to return to continue the conflict and work out his mighty play of God's providence among the nations.

What marvelous unfolding of the secrets of the universe this scene affords! How we see the wheels within the wheels and over all, the hand of a man controlling! Let us not henceforth be perplexed when our prayer seems to delay or our blessings linger. Let us understand a little how much it costs to bring the least gift to earth from heaven, even through the legions of the enemy! Once when David was thirsting for the water from his own well at Bethlehem, three brave soldiers of his band broke through the ranks of the foe and, covered with blood, brought back the coveted water. David's heart was deeply touched, so much so that he could not drink the water they had brought but poured it out before the Lord saying, "Is it not the blood of men who went at the risk of their lives?" (2 Samuel 23:17). So every cup of water that we drink has required that someone should break through the legions of darkness to bring it to us. Our blessed Master has led the brave assault, and many mighty and loving angels are still maintaining the conflict against the hosts of evil and guarding our interests against the powers of earth and hell.

Oh, how our hearts will burst with grateful transport some day when we see with the quickened vision of eternity how much our blessings have cost and how hard-won the battle of our salvation has been! Let us not be discouraged if sometimes the conflict lasts longer than a day, a week or a month; if it be the battle of the Lord it is always victory at last, and faith can lift aloft her banner from the beginning and shout "Jehovah-nissi." "But thanks be to God! He gives us the victory through our Lord Jesus Christ" (1 Corinthians 15:57).

Such was Daniel's prayer and the immediate circumstances that followed it. The subsequent history of Israel is the unfolding of the answer. Glorious indeed, perhaps beyond all that he had dreamed, was the fulfillment! While he was kneeling in his silent closet, God was touching the heart of this king and emperor in the very flash of his imperial triumph with the strangest thought that ever came to heathen man—the purpose to restore the captive Jews to their ancient home. The proclamation soon followed which publicly announced to all Cyrus' realm that the God of heaven had commanded him to fulfill this great task and rebuild the city of Jerusalem.

Perhaps Daniel never saw that stirring scene as 50,000 exiles moved across the desert to their ancient home, and, through miracles of faith and providence, under Zerubbabel, Joshua, Ezra and Nehemiah, rebuilt their temple and their city and reared out of the ruins of two generations their national life once more, restoring the line through which their glorious King was at length to come. But some day God let him know that this procession of glorious results was the answer to his simple prayer and the recompense to his tears and his trust.

And so, though we may not see on earth all the glorious issues of our waiting years and hours of spiritual conflict and believing intercession, yet some day we, too, will see the glorious harvest which has planted the heavens and covered the earth. We will know that the greatest of all ministries is not eloquent speech, or munificent beneficence, or profound wisdom or untiring work, but the still hour, the touch of faith, the whisper of prayer, the silent ministry, that moves the hand that moves the universe.

The Promise of Faith

To Daniel's faith was given the most glorious of all messages—the revelation of the first and second comings of the Lord Jesus Christ. The very date of His first was so definitely unfolded to him that it has ever since seemed incredible that any Jew could question the identity of the true Messiah. But far beyond this glorious message the light of promise shone into the ages yet to come, revealing the sequence of the world's empires and providential developments, the scenes and incidents of human history until the last time, and marking for those who rightly read the scroll of prophecy with a light which is growing clearer and plainer as the time draws near, even the period of the last crisis with the lights and shadows of glory and of tribulation which will blend so luridly in the day of the Lord. Best of all Daniel knew that his people would be delivered in that awful crisis, and that his part should be kept safe in the eternal light and recompense. Much of the vision to him was sealed; but he knew that he should rest and stand in his lot at the end of the days.

So still to faith is given the promise of His coming and the glorious hopes of the future. There is a generation which will not die but will be changed in a moment at His appearing. There is a generation that will know this by faith and will be found looking up because their redemption draws near. Perhaps none of us can yet say that we live in that generation, but we can all accept the blessed hope, and if we truly learn the lessons of Daniel's faith, to us may be given in due time His own last reward, the promise that our eyes "will see the Son of Man coming in clouds with great power and glory" (Mark 13:26).

Oh, let us be true to the purpose of faith, steadfast in the proving of faith, obedient to the prayer of faith; and we will receive the promise of faith in all the fullness of His will for us and all the glory of His great salvation.

CHAPTER 18

Christ

The Author and Perfecter of Our Faith

> *Therefore, since we are surrounded by such a great cloud of witnesses, let us throw off everything that hinders and the sin that so easily entangles, and let us run with perseverance the race marked out for us. Let us fix our eyes on Jesus, the author and perfecter of our faith, who for the joy set before him endured the cross, scorning its shame, and he sat down at the right hand of the throne of God. (Hebrews 12:1-2)*

Thus the apostle sums up the illustrious patterns of faith which we have for some time been contemplating in the firmament of scriptural character. They shine like a constellation of stars, a Milky Way across the face of the past, radiant with spiritual glory. But the catalog is not complete until the starry train is closed with a still more glorious luminary, the Bright and Morning

Star, Jesus Himself, the Author and Perfecter of our faith, or rather the Princely Leader and Supreme Pattern, as well as the Author and Perfecter of our faith.

Christ, Our Pattern of Faith

We are so accustomed to think of Jesus in His higher character and divine nature, as lifted by His deity far above all our infirmities and struggles, that we are in danger of forgetting the lesson of His literal humanity and His absolute dependence upon His Father for all His life and work, through the same channels and methods of communion and support as the weakest of His disciples possessed.

On the one hand we must guard against the error of the Unitarian and ever recognize and honor His Supreme Godhead and equal glory with the Father. Yet, on the other hand, we must remember that every error has some truth back of it, and that Unitarianism is but an effort in some measure of the spiritual sense to emphasize the real humanity of Christ and that the Church has at least failed to fully realize that while the Son was in the form of God equal with God, yet He "did not consider equality with God something to be grasped, but made himself nothing, taking the very nature of a servant, being made in human likeness" (Philippians 2:6-7) in the most complete and literal sense. In short, He suspended for the time the exercise of His absolute powers as the Deity, and took the

place of dependence, subordinating Himself to
God as a creature for the support of every mo-
ment and the supply of everything, exactly as we
His children are dependent upon Him.

We sometimes forget that Christ was "tempted
in every way, just as we are" (Hebrews 4:15), and
that "since the children have flesh and blood, he
too shared in their humanity" (2:14); being "made
like his brothers in every way, in order that he
might become a merciful and faithful high priest
in service to God. . . . Because he himself suffered
when he was tempted, he is able to help those
who are being tempted" (2:17-18). His childhood
was a perfectly human growth, and His spiritual
life developed through the grace of God. "[Jesus]
grew and became strong; he was filled with wisdom, and the grace of God was upon him" (Luke
2:40).

In His conflict with Satan in the wilderness He
refused to take the place of independence and
work a miracle to relieve His sufferings as the
devil sought to instigate Him to do. But He
voluntarily chose to leave Himself in His Father's
hands as an ordinary man and expected the same
provision for His protection and support as God
had appointed unto man, exclaiming, "It is written: 'Man does not live on bread alone, but on
every word that comes from the mouth of God' "
(Matthew 4:4).

Throughout His whole earthly life we find
Him uniformly confessing:

For I have come down from heaven not to do my will but to do the will of him who sent me. (John 6:38)

By myself I can do nothing. (5:30)

These words you hear are not my own; they belong to the Father who sent me. (14:24)

The one who sent me is with me; he has not left me alone, for I always do what pleases him. (8:29)

Just as the living Father sent me and I live because of the Father, so the one who feeds on me will live because of me. (6:57)

He did not begin His public ministry until He had been specially endued for His work by the power of the Holy Spirit, and He ever recognized the Spirit as the Source and Author of all His work. He lived a life of prayer. In all the great emergencies of His earthly life He committed Himself implicitly and trustfully to the care and love of His Father, as we are required to do.

Thus His whole life was one of dependence, and dependence is just another word for faith. Faith just means God in a human life, the supernatural rather than the natural. He Himself attributed His miracles to the exercise of faith. When the fruitless fig tree withered away and His disciples wondered, He simply answered, "Have faith in God" (Mark

11:22), implying that this was the secret of the miracle. When He stood beside the grave of Lazarus, He believed and thanked the Father for the answer before it came. The dramatic pictures of His inner life and sufferings in the final conflict of the cross, which are given us in the Psalms and prophecies, afford a sublime picture of faith. We see it sorely pressed by the clouds of sorrow and temptation, until even the bitter cry is extorted, "My God, my God, why have you forsaken me?" (Matthew 27:46). But we also see the triumph of faith as He cries in the 22nd Psalm, "In you our fathers put their trust; . . . and were not disappointed. . . . From you comes the theme of my praise in the great assembly" (Psalm 22:4-5, 25). Likewise in the 50th chapter of Isaiah, He exclaims, "Because the Sovereign LORD helps me, I will not be disgraced. Therefore have I set my face like flint, and I know I will not be put to shame" (Isaiah 50:7).

This is the language of trust and victory, and it was through this faith, as we are told in the passage in Hebrews, that in His last agony, "Jesus, . . . for the joy set before him endured the cross, scorning its shame" (12:2). His life was a life of faith; His death was a victory of faith; His resurrection was a triumph of faith; His mediatorial reign is all one long victory of faith. "Since that time he waits for his enemies to be made his footstool" (10:13).

And so for us He has become the pattern of faith, and in every situation of difficulty, temptation and distress He has gone before us waving the banner of trust and triumph, bidding us to follow in His victorious footsteps. He is the great Pattern Believer. While we must claim our salvation by faith, the Great Forerunner also claimed the world's salvation by the same faith.

Let us, therefore, consider this glorious Leader henceforth, as perhaps we have not done before, as in all points our perfect example; and as we follow close behind Him, let us remember where He has triumphed we may triumph too.

> Our glorious Leader claims our praise,
> For His own pattern given;
> While the long cloud of witnesses
> Show the same path to Heaven.

Christ, the Author of Our Faith

Herein lies the immeasurable distance between the Old Testament and the New; the Old is light but the New is power. The lives of Abraham, David, Elijah, Daniel, are glorious examples, but they are impotent to quicken our helpless spirits into the life which animated them. We see them climbing the heights of faith and holy achievement until they are almost lost to view in the heavenly altitudes of their illustrious goal. But they seem to stand afar and paralyze our helplessness by the very height of their attainments, which only discourages our feeble and unequal energies. We can admire their surpassing excellence, but only feel more keenly our inferiority and inability to follow. Example alone cannot elevate human character and life beyond a fixed limitation. It can exalt our ideal, it can inspire our ambition, but it cannot energize our moral and spiritual weakness.

But Jesus Christ is infinitely more than an example. He has not come to stand upon the heights of supreme attainment and call to us in the valley below, saying, "Follow me." But having traversed all the pathway of conflict and progress and marked every step in which we are called to follow, He comes down to our level to take us by the hand and lead us upward with His own strong arm, inspiring in us His own faith, enduing us with His own might and crowning us with victory which we will feel is all His own.

He is not only the Pattern, but He is the Power of faith for all who so receive Him. In many subordinate senses this is true. He is the One who has given us the promises as the foundation and encouragement of our faith and made them so explicit, so unequivocal, so full of encouragement and certainty that there is no room for hesitation or doubt on the part of any candid heart. He is the One who has confirmed the promises by His own redeeming work becoming their Surety, fulfilling all their conditions, meeting the requirements which we could not meet for their fulfillment, and then claiming them for us as for Himself, so that "No matter how many promises God has made, they are 'yes' in Christ. And so through him the 'Amen' is spoken by us to the glory of God" (2 Corinthians 1:20). He is the One who has obtained for us the promise of the Spirit to help our infirmities, to quicken our spiritual life, to breathe in our hearts the new life of God which is the soil of faith and every grace.

But beyond all this, in a sense more direct and supernatural, Christ is the Author of our faith in this glorious sense that He so unites Himself with us and dwells in us as a living personality that He imparts His own very faith to our spirit. He enables us in His life, light and quickening presence to see the promises as He sees them, to claim them as He claims them, to believe as He believes, to trust with His own perfect trustfulness and to repose in His Father's love and faithfulness with the same heavenly confidence and filial faith which He Himself ever exemplified in His own earthly life. As in every respect He gives Himself to us, so nonetheless does He do so in respect to faith, and we can say, literally and truly, we have yielded up our own poor, imperfect faith and love and received Him as our perfect substitute. "I no longer live, but Christ lives in me. The life I live in the body, I live by faith in the Son of God, who loved me and gave himself for me" (Galatians 2:20).

This was His own command to His disciples. When they wondered at the power of His faith, He met their marveling by offering them the same power and commanding them to have faith in God. Oh, the infinite and everlasting rest of ceasing from the struggles of our own weak and doubting hearts, and entering into His life and peace and trust! Blessed Captain of our salvation! He has not furnished all the heavenly chain and left the last golden link for our weak hands to forge, but to our weak hearts and hands on this side as surely as to the eternal throne on the heaven side He supplies and fastens the strong cable of His faithful promises.

It was Tantalus of old who spread the table and held forth the vessels of tempting fruits and viands to the starving victim, bound and helpless, and able to reach out only an arm's length less than the space that separated the tempting gifts. It was agony to know that relief was offered so near and yet could not be grasped. Christ does not mock us with His mighty promises and matchless grace in this way; but His arm reaches all the way until it touches our weak, paralyzed hands, and taking hold of them, teaches them in turn to meet His grasp and claim His glorious praises. Not only does He do His glorious part but He enables us likewise to do our part. And as we respond to His touch and cooperate with His grace, the hands of Christ hold our weak, trembling hands and teach us to trust and pray in the faith of God. *Blessed Author of our faith! You are indeed our All in all, and faith itself must lay her crown at last at Your blessed feet.*

Christ, the Perfecter of Our Faith

This expression is intended to include the whole discipline of faith through which our

Master leads us as He tests and develops, enlarges and establishes the faith which He Himself has given. Every gift and grace of God is susceptible of boundless improvement, and as we meet Him in the school of life we grow up into Him in all things and reach at length the fullness of the stature of perfect men in Christ. This is especially true of faith. All through the Bible we read of the need to suffer "in all kinds of trials. These have come so that your faith—of greater worth than gold, which perishes even though refined by fire" (1 Peter 1:6-7). This chapter especially unfolds the principles of spiritual discipline and teaches us that God deals with us as sons, and designs all the sufferings of our earthly pilgrimage to be an education for our souls and to deepen and strengthen our spiritual character. But it is indispensable, in order to get this result, that we meet all these trials in the spirit of faith.

Suffering in itself is not sanctifying but depressing, especially to a doubting and discouraged heart. It is only when we meet it as the Master met it, in the spirit of joyous triumph, that we can meet it in victory and turn it to good account. The key to victorious suffering is given in our text, "who for the joy set before him endured the cross, scorning its shame, and sat down at the right hand of the throne of God" (Hebrews 12:2). He entered the valley of sorrow with His eye far beyond it, piercing all the clouds that encompassed Him and contemplating only the glory that absorbed His vision on the resurrection side, and so His sorrow was as if it were not and His shame was despised in the prospect of the eternal glory to which it led.

And so for us the keynote is, "strengthen your feeble arms and weak knees" (12:12). "Throw off everything that hinders . . . do not lose heart when he rebukes you, because the Lord disciplines those he loves" (12:1, 5-6). Thus will sorrow be disarmed and evil be transformed into a messenger of God and a teacher of faith in the school of Christ.

It is a blessed and inspiring lesson to recognize every trial and difficulty as it meets us, not as an enemy that has come to overwhelm us, but as a divine opportunity to prove something more in the all-sufficiency of Christ, and to show something more through which faith can carry us in victory. Then will all earth's mountains become a way, and Satan's stumbling blocks stones with which to build a stairway up to heaven.

The School of Faith

We have seen in the survey of the lives and characters which we have been contemplating how varied the faith through which God's wisdom leads His children and the lessons in which He educates them. These Old Testament biographies are but samples in the school of faith in which Christ is graduating His disciples still. And it would be little credit to the light and blessing of the New Testament dispensation if the twilight ages of the past should surpass in their examples of faith and power the full glory of the Christian age and Pentecostal dispensation. "God had planned something better for us so that only together with us would they be made perfect" (11:40). "(for the law made nothing perfect), and a better hope is introduced, by which we draw near to God" (7:19). Christ's great purpose for His people is to train them to know the hope of their calling, and "the riches of his glorious inheritance in the saints, and his incomparably great power for [those] who believe" (Ephesians 1:18-19).

Let us prove in all our varied walks of life and scenes of conflict the fullness of His power and grace, and thus will we show "in the coming ages . . . the incomparable riches of his grace, expressed in his kindness to us in Christ Jesus" (2:7).

Friend, are you following your Teacher in the school of faith and finishing the education which is to fit you for "an eternal glory that far outweighs them all" (2 Corinthians 4:17)?

This is only the school of faith. The ages to come will furnish the boundless field for its eternal and glorious achievements.

Little can we now dream what these lessons will mean for us some day when we will sit with Him on His throne and share with Him the power of God and the government of the universe. Let us be faithful scholars now and soon with Him we too will have endured the cross, scorned the shame, and will sit "down at the right hand of the throne of God" (Hebrews 12:2).